EASY TO MAKE
SEWING

EASY TO MAKE
SEWING

Wendy Gardiner

ANAYA PUBLISHERS LTD LONDON

First published in Great Britain in 1992
by Anaya Publishers Ltd, Strode House,
44–50 Osnaburgh Street, London NW1 3ND

Design by Design 23
Photography: Steve Tanner
Illustrator: Terry Evans

British Library Cataloguing in Publication Data

Gardiner, Wendy
Easy to make: Sewing – (Easy to make)
I. Title II. Series
745.59
ISBN 1 85470 130 4

Typeset by Servis Filmsetting Ltd, Manchester, UK
Colour reproduction by Columbia Offset, Singapore
Printed and bound in Hong Kong

CONTENTS

Introduction

When something is handmade it is always extra-special, which is why sewing is not just a relaxing hobby providing hours of enjoyment, but is also a chance to create something personal.

The projects included in *Easy to Make: Sewing*, have been specifically designed to appeal to a wide range of sewers – from busy mums who love to sew but lack time, to dedicated sewers looking for something new.

For the inexperienced or those whose time is at a premium, making things for the home can provide just the right amount of sewing as well as adding those special personal finishing touches to the decor.

Even those with limited ability need not be daunted. The simple step-by-step instructions guide you through the construction from making the pattern to adding the final stitch. And, ever-conscious of time and tight budgets, each of the projects can be completed from start to finish in a short period of time, at a minimal cost.

The techniques described in this book include many of the latest shortcuts and professional sewing tips. Gone are the days when sewing was a time-consuming chore; it really can be fun, quick and easy. And it couldn't be simpler; the materials required are listed at the beginning of each project. Many can be made from fabric remnants – it's worth raiding your work-box to find those treasured scraps that you refused to discard.

The Better Techniques, at the back of the book, include basic guidelines on equipment, stitching techniques, types of seam and seam finishes and other information that will help you achieve perfect results every time. If in doubt about any technique, take time to read this chapter before you begin, and so avoid any possible pitfalls.

All the measurements in this book have been expressed in both imperial and metric units. However the conversions used have been simplified and so are not exact. It is therefore advisable to follow one or the other of the measurement systems and not to mix them within a project.

With over 30 projects to choose from there is something for every occasion: the Quick Quick Sew chapter includes six projects that can be made in a minimum of time. Transform a room in minutes with the 30-minute cushions and a quick close-fitting window treatment. The timely tote bag makes a great gift idea and the cook's apron can be made ready for the barbecue tonight!

Brighten up breakfast with the sunshine table set. The primary colours and painted faces will add a glimmer of cheer to the murkiest of mornings. This chapter also includes a choice of gift ideas that are economical to make and yet will give great pleasure. Tiny tots are not forgotten in Small Talk, as fun at playtime is ensured with the playmat whilst the colourful cot safe bumper adds a wall of protection to baby's cot. Pack a perfect picnic with the Al fresco picnic set and reversible chair cushions.

The chapter Fun with Fabric aims to inspire, from a pretty and practical sewing caddy to an imaginative wall hanging where you can indulge your creative urge.

Finally bring festive cheer to winter nights and count down to Christmas with our advent calendar. The holiday tablecloth has pockets in which to tuck hidden surprise presents.

Once started on the wonderful art of sewing for pleasure you will find the choices unlimited – a different fabric, change of appliqué or added embroidery will enable you to continue creating original gifts and new ideas for many years.

ONE

Quick Quick Sew

30-minute cushions

Make either one of these comfortable cushions in a matter of minutes. Each one needs only a small amount of material so they are economical as well as speedy to sew.

Materials for bolster cushion
½yd (50cm) of 36in (90cm) wide fabric
1⅛yd (1m) of ⅝in (1.5cm) wide ribbon
Bolster cushion pad

Materials for square cushion
⅝yd (60cm) of 54in (140cm) wide fabric
16in (40cm) square cushion pad

Bolster cushion
1 If necessary, cut the fabric to measure 20 × 36in (50 × 90cm). Then, turn both short ends under 4in (10cm), turning the raw edge under again ½in (1.25cm). Machine-stitch in place close to the turned edge and again 1in (2.5cm) from the first row to form the ribbon casing.

2 Fold the fabric in half lengthways, with right sides together and machine-stitch, leaving the ribbon casings free. To do this, stitch to the first casing, leave seam of casing section unstitched, stitch to the casing at the other end of the cushion cover, leave the casing free and then stitch to the end.

3 Press the seam and turn through to the right side. Cut the ribbon into two equal lengths and thread through the casings at either end. Finally, insert the bolster cushion before pulling the ribbon ties tightly, gathering each end. Finish with a firmly knotted bow.

Square cushion
1 Cut fabric to 21 × 46in (53 × 116cm). Neaten the short ends by turning under ⅜in (1cm) and then again, encasing the raw edges, and machine-stitching.

2 With right sides together, fold the ends to the centre and overlap by 4in (10cm) so that the overall width is 20in (50cm). Machine-stitch both side seams. Neaten and trim the raw edges and then turn through and press.

3 Finish with a machine-stitched decorative border 2in (5cm) from the outer edge all around the cushion cover.

NB: The overlapped edges should be sufficient to hold the cushion securely in place. However, a Velcro spot can be added to the centre back opening if desired.

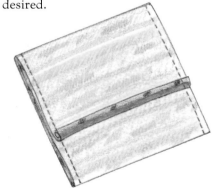

Overlap the ends, making the overall width 20in (50cm).

Timely tote bag

Lightweight but roomy, with a handy inside pocket, this timely tote will make a great gift. The wax-covered cotton is also waterproof, making it doubly useful.

Materials
$\frac{3}{4}$yd (70cm) of 36in (90cm) wide waxed
    cotton fabric
5in (12cm) of Velcro

Making the bag
1 Fold the fabric in half, selvedge to selvedge with right sides together. Following the cutting layout cut 2 main pieces 15 × 17in (38 × 43cm); 2 facings 15 × 3in (38 × 8cm); 2 handles 3½ × 16in (9 × 41cm) and 1 pocket section placed on the fold 5in (13cm) square.

2 Unfold the pocket section and then turn under ½in (1cm) at one end. On the wrong side machine-stitch one strip of Velcro over the turned edge. Stitch the other half of the Velcro to the wrong side of the other end of the pocket section ½in (1cm) from the raw edge.

3 Fold the pocket so that the Velcro strips meet and there is a ½in (1cm) lip on the back of the pocket. Stitch the side seams (if using a fabric other than wax-covered cotton, stitch seams with right sides together and then turn through).

4 Fold the handles in half lengthways, right sides together, machine-stitch the long edge and turn through. Then top stitch ¼in (6mm) from both side edges before pinning the ends of the handles to the top right side of the bag sections. Place them 4in (10cm) from the side edges and then machine-stitch in place.

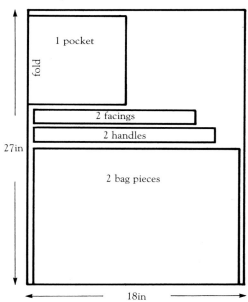

Fabric layout

27in

18in

1 pocket

fold

2 facings

2 handles

2 bag pieces

12

5 Pin the bag front to the back, with right sides together. Machine-stitch both side seams and across the bottom.

```
┌─────────────────────────┐
│░░░░░░░░░░░░░░░░░░░░░░░░░░░│
│    Velcro strip         │
│                         │
│   POCKET SECTION        │
│                         │
│    Velcro strip         │
│░░░░░░░░░░░░░░░░░░░░░░░░░░░│
└─────────────────────────┘
```

6 Stitch the facings together end to end. Next, pin and stitch the facings to the top of the bag, right sides together and matching side seams with facing seams. Still working with the bag inside out, turn facings out to the wrong side of the bag, pressing the raw edges under $\frac{1}{2}$in (1cm).

7 Pin the pocket lip under the facing below one handle so that the top of the pocket with the Velcro closure butts up against the facing edge. Finally, top-stitch the facing to the bag close to the turned edge, catching the pocket lip as you go.

Cook's cover apron

This brightly coloured, no-nonsense apron is perfect for the busy cook, and accidental spills and splashes are easily wiped from the versatile chintz fabric.

Materials

¾yd (70cm) of 36in (90cm) wide cotton chintz or waxed cotton

2¼yd (2.10m) of 1in (2.5cm) wide grosgrain ribbon

Making the apron

1 Cut two rectangles for this basic shaped apron. The bib measures 10in (26cm) wide × 12in (30cm) deep and the skirt 26in (66cm) wide × 22in (56cm) deep. For the neck loop, ties and decorative trim, cut the ribbon as follows: neck loop 23 in (58cm) long; 2 waist ties, each 17in (43cm) long; 2 decorative trims, one 15in (38cm) and finally one 9in (23cm) long.

2 Starting with the bib, hem either side edge by turning in ¼in (6mm) twice and machine-stitching. Fold one end under ½in (1cm), then a further 1½in (4cm) and pin in place. Then with the right side facing, machine-stitch this end with three rows of top stitching in a contrasting coloured thread.

3 Next, join the bib to the skirt with the right sides together. Pin the unstitched edge of the bib to the centre of one long edge of the skirt. Machine-stitch 1in (2.5cm) from the edges. Open out the apron and press.

4 With the wrong side facing, turn the seam allowance and remainder of top edge under ½in (1.25cm) twice and pin in place before machine-stitching right across from side edge to side edge.

5 Pin the ribbon strips diagonally across the bottom left corner of the skirt, trimming the ends to match the side edges. Machine-stitch in place down either side of both ribbon trims. Then hem both side edges of the skirt encasing the ribbon ends at the same time.

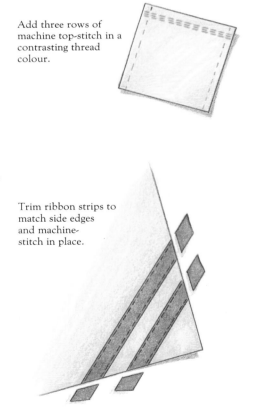

Add three rows of machine top-stitch in a contrasting thread colour.

Trim ribbon strips to match side edges and machine-stitch in place.

6 Finish the bottom edge by folding it under ½in (1.25cm), then a further 1½in (4cm). With the right side facing, top-stitch 4 rows of stitching in contrasting thread, approximately 1in (2.5cm) from the lower edge.

7 Finally, add the ties and neck loop. Turn the ribbon ends under ¼in (6mm) and pin to the wrong side of the top edge of bib and either side edge. Machine-stitch, following the previous line of stitching and close to the outer edge.

Close-fitting window treatment

This close-fitting curtain is quickly made and fitted. The simple design uses the minimum of fabric providing a highly economical way to dress small windows effectively.

Materials

Main fabric: calculate amount needed by measuring window width and height from the outer edge of the frame, then add 1in (2.5cm) seam allowance to both measurements.

Lining: same size as the main fabric

Stick and Sew Velcro: the width of the window plus an extra 3in (8cm)

1 popper

Making the curtain

1 Cut both main fabric and lining to the size calculated. Cut a length of the Velcro to the same width as the fabric and 2 pieces each 1½in (4cm) long.

2 Pin the lining to the main fabric, right sides together, and machine-stitch ½in (1cm) from the edge leaving a turning gap at the top edge. Neaten the seam allowance, turn through and press. Slipstitch the opening.

3 Pin the sew-in half of the Velcro strip to the top edge on the lining side and machine-stitch in place. Stitch one of the 1½in (4cm) Velcro pieces to the lining at the bottom of the left side. Working on the right side, top-stitch around the curtain, approximately 1in (2.5cm) from the edge.

4 With the right side uppermost, fold the bottom right corner back to the left side so that the corner point is level with the side edge. Hand sew a popper to the

Shaded area indicates position of Velcro strips.

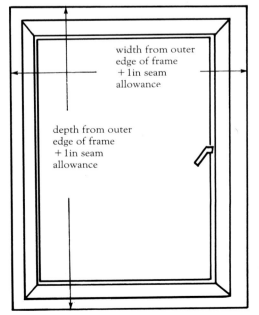

width from outer edge of frame + 1in seam allowance

depth from outer edge of frame + 1in seam allowance

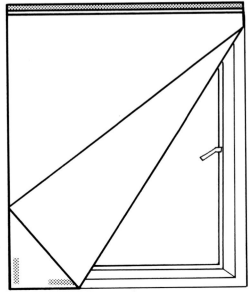

side edge and the other half to the corner to hold in place. Stitch the remaining 1½in (4cm) Velcro piece to the bottom edge, on the lining side, at the point where the curtain folds back.

5 Finally stick the adhesive half of the Velcro to the top of the window frame, and each of the small pieces to the left edge and bottom frame to correspond with the Velcro on the curtain.

Delightful window dressing

Create the illusion of an unusual-shaped window with these softly draped curtains. The classic style is looped back to conceal an ordinary rectangular window.

Materials
Fine cotton fabric, see below for amount.

Making the curtains
1 Measure the height of the window from the pole at the top to the bottom edge of the window frame. Then add 3½in (9cm) extra to the height for the pole casing and 5in (13cm) for the hem – a total of 8½in (22cm). Measure the width, starting 2in (5cm) beyond the window frame on either side. Add an extra 2in (5cm) for the seam allowances and then multiply the total width measurement by 2 for a full-gathered effect.

2 The width can be made up of a number of lengths (drops) to obtain the total width: here, 2 lengths (drops) of 45in (115cm) wide fabric are used. Once the measurements are known, calculate the amount of fabric required. To do this, multiply the height by the number of lengths required to make the total width eg: 59½in (152cm) × 4 widths = 6⅝yd (6.08m).

3 Cut the fabric into equal lengths as determined by the height (drop). If two or more are needed for each side, machine-stitch them together. For sheer fabrics, use a French seam which neatly encloses all raw edges.

Working the design
4 Hem the curtains by turning the ends under 2½in (6cm) twice and machine-stitch close to the turning. Narrow hem one side edge of each curtain.

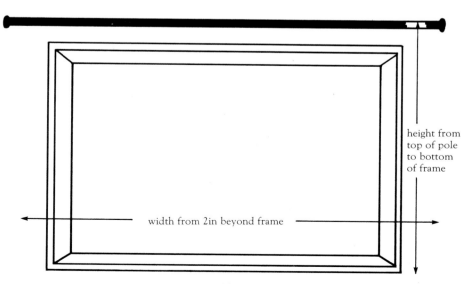

height from
top of pole
to bottom
of frame

width from 2in beyond frame

5 For this draped design, the curtains are joined in the centre at the top. To do this, machine-stitch the remaining unstitched edges of each side, right sides together from the top edge for approximately 8in (20cm). Press the seam open.

6 On the wrong side, hem the centre edges by turning the raw edge under ¼in (6mm) and again another ¼in (6mm). Stitch close to the turned edge.

7 Make the pole casing by folding the top edge under ½in (1.25cm) to the wrong side and again 3in (8cm). Machine-stitch close to the turned edge.

8 Slide the finished curtain onto the curtain pole, adjusting the gathers as you go. If desired, run a gathering stitch along the top stitching line to permanently gather the curtains.

9 To form the softly draped effect take hold of the centre front edge of either side approximately halfway down and hook it loosely over the pole end or a strategically placed hook.

TWO

Around the Kitchen

Sunshine table set

*Brighten the day with this sunny placemat and coaster table set.
Made from cotton, they are easily laundered so ideal
for everyday use at breakfast time.*

Materials for six placemats
1⅜ yd (1.30m) of 36in (90cm) wide yellow
cotton
Red, white and blue fabric remnants for
face
6 yd (5.50m) orange bias binding
Orange and black thread
Interfacing
¾yd (70cm) of wadding

Materials for six coasters
11in (28cm) of 36in (90cm) wide cotton
poplin
11in (28cm) of 36in (90cm) wide white
cotton poplin
Interfacing
For the face: fabric scraps and
embroidery threads

Making the placemats
1 Fold the yellow cotton in half
crossways. Draw around an upturned
plate or bowl, approximately 12in (30cm)
diameter, adding 2in (5cm) seam
allowances. Cut two pieces for each
placemat. Interface both sections. Cut
eyes and mouth from fabric remnants.

2 Bond the eyes and mouth to the right
side of one circle and zigzag-stitch around
the edges to secure in place. Using black
thread, add two French knots for the
nose and zigzag-stitch the eyebrows.

3 Quilt the back section of each
placemat (for quick and easy quilting, use
an interfacing with ready-printed quilting
lines such as Quiltex). Cut a circle of
wadding for each mat, again using the
plate as a template. Pin the wadding in
place over the quilted interfacing.

4 Add the appliquéd front, sandwiching
the wadding and with the face facing
uppermost. Machine-stitch through all
thicknesses all round. Trim the seam
allowance to within a scant ¼in (6mm) of
the stitching, clipping occasionally to aid
shaping.

5 Using bright orange thread, zigzag-
stitch the curved sun rays around the
edge, each approximately 1½in (4cm) long.
Finally, open out and pin the orange bias
binding around the edge, working with
the face side uppermost. Machine-stitch
in place and then turn the binding over
to the back, encasing the raw edges and
slipstitch in place.

Making the coasters
1 To make the coasters, fold the fabric in
half in order to cut two layers at a time.
Using a large cup or saucer as a template,
draw around the cup, adding a further ½in
•(1.25cm) seam allowance all the way
round. Cut 2 pieces for each coaster and
interface both layers.

2 For the face, cut the yawning mouth
from red poplin, bond in place and
secure with satin stitch. Add the
eyebrows, using a zigzag stitch and then
hand sew the eyelids and lashes. Finish
the face with two French knots to form
the nostrils.

3 Pin the plain circle to the face section,
with right sides together. Machine-stitch
½in (1.25cm) from the edge, leaving a
turning gap. Trim and clip the seam
allowance then turn through to right side.
Slipstitch the opening.

4 Make the clouds from the white poplin. Again, fold the fabric in half so that the two layers are cut at the same time. Using tailor's chalk or a soft pencil, draw some cloud shapes. Cut two layers for each cloud, and interface both layers as before.

5 Machine-stitch the two pieces with right sides together, turn through and press. Pin the cloud to the coaster on the left side and then top-stitch around the cloud edges attaching it to the coaster at the same time. Add some cloud shaping if desired, again by top-stitching.

Napkins and rings

These nifty napkins are quick and easy even for the complete novice. Made from squares of cotton, they are simply stitched and trimmed. Matching napkin rings add the finishing touch.

Materials for six napkins
½yd (50cm) of 45in (115cm) wide yellow cotton
½yd (50cm) of 45in (115cm) wide white cotton
Yellow and white fabric paints

Materials for six napkin rings
Remnant of white cotton fabric
Remnant of yellow cotton fabric
Heavyweight interfacing
7½in (19cm) of ¾in (2cm) wide Velcro

Making the napkins
1 Cut three 15in (38cm) squares from both pieces of cotton fabric. Fold each in half and then into quarters.

2 Draw two scallop shapes on the outer edge. Open out fabric.

3 Work a straight machine-stitch around the scallop shapes, to prevent the fabric from stretching, using white thread on the yellow napkins and yellow thread on the white. Then stitch again with a close zigzag-stitch, going over the first line of straight-stitching.

4 Using small embroidery scissors, trim the napkin very close to the stitching being careful not to cut the stitches. Press the edges with a damp cloth.

5 Finish each napkin with a sleepy face above one scallop. Draw lightly with tailor's chalk or pencil and paint over with fabric paint. Use white paint on the yellow napkins and yellow paint on the white.

Making the napkin rings
1 Using the template, cut 2 cloud pieces for each napkin ring. Each cloud requires a piece of fabric 4 × 8in (10 × 20cm). From the yellow cotton fabric cut one strip measuring 4in (10cm) wide × 7½in (19cm) long for each ring.

2 Cut 1 piece of the heavyweight interfacing for each cloud, again using the template for size. Then for the rings, cut a narrow strip 1½ × 6½in (4 × 17cm).

3 Fold the fabric strip in half lengthways, with right sides together and stitch the side seam. Refold the strip so that the seam is in the middle and then place the interfacing over the centre. Machine-stitch across one end, catching the end of the interfacing within the seam.

4 Turn the strip through to the right side before tucking in approximately ½in (1.25cm) of the unstitched ends to the inside. Pin in place and press firmly.

Stitch Velcro to the cloud, and end of strip.

5 For the cloud, pin the interfacing to the wrong side of one cloud piece. Add the remaining cloud section, sandwiching the interfacing. Machine-stitch around the edge using straight stitch. Then zigzag stitch over the edges all the way around to neaten.

6 Machine-stitch the pinned end of a strip to the centre of each cloud base with the seam of the strip facing uppermost.

7 With the cloud and attached strip still facing uppermost, cut a 1¼in (3cm) length of Velcro. Pin, then stitch, one half to the cloud just above the strip.

8 To finish, turn the napkin ring over and stitch the remaining half of the Velcro to the opposite end of the strip. When completed, fold the strip over into a ring, so that the Velcro joins, and the ring sits on the cloud base.

NAPKIN RING

French bread bag

Cook up an international flavour and keep delicious bread fresh for longer in this brightly-decorated French bread bag. It will add a splash of colour to any kitchen.

Materials
½yd (50cm) cotton chintz
20in (51cm) thick red cord
Remnants of red, white and blue cotton

Making the bag
1 Cut 2 pieces of cotton chintz measuring 26 × 7in (66 × 18cm). For the decorative flag, cut a strip 2¼ × 11in (6 × 28cm) each in red, blue and white cotton.

2 Turn both long edges of each strip under ½in (1.25cm) and press to form crisp edge. Pin the red strip diagonally across the right side of one bag section, starting 1½in (4cm) from the bottom edge. Pin the white strip above this, overlapping the edges, and finally add the blue strip, again overlapping the edges. Machine-stitch in matching thread to hold in place, then trim the side edges of the strips to match the side edges of the bag.

3 With the right sides together, pin the front to the back bag section. Starting at the top right side, machine-stitch for 3½in (9cm). Leave a 1in (2.5cm) gap unstitched for the cord casing, then continue down the side seam, across the diagonal strips to the end. Stitch the left side in the same manner, continuing across the bottom.

Position red strip first, then white above it, then the blue.

With right sides together stitch back and front sections together.

26

4 Turn the top edge under ½in (1.25cm) and press. Fold the top in again a further 2in (5cm) so that the pressed edge is just below the level of the gaps in the side seams and then machine-stitch in place. Machine a second row of stitching 1in (2.5cm) from the top edge to form the cord casing.

5 Turn the bag to the right side and finish by threading the red cord through the casing.

Cozy casserole coat

Keep delicious dishes warm with this cozy casserole coat. The simple design can be adapted to any dish shape – making an attractive and practical addition to the dinner table.

Materials

¾yd (70cm) of 36in (90cm) wide medium-weight fabric *or* remnant to suit

Quilted interfacing or 4oz (200g) wadding

Making the coat

1 To measure the dish to determine the size of the coat required, first measure across the width of the base plus the height of the sides and then the length of the base including the height of the sides. Add ¾in (2cm) seam allowance to both measurements to determine the size of the coat pattern. Fold the fabric in half and cut 2 pieces to the size required. Cut a piece of quilted interfacing or wadding to the same size.

2 To make the ties, cut 8 strips each 1 × 3in (2.5 × 7.5cm). With right sides together sew the long edge and across one end. Turn through to the right side and press.

3 Lay the ties across the right side of one main piece, matching the raw edge to the side edge, 2in (5cm) from the corners so that each corner has two ties. Stitch in place and then fold all the ties to the centre of the main piece to prevent the loose ends catching in the side seams.

4 Pin the wadding or quilted interfacing to the wrong side of the remaining back section and quilt in place. Then pin the back to the front with right sides together, sandwiching the ties.

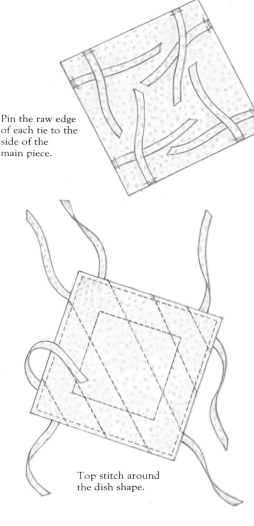

Pin the raw edge of each tie to the side of the main piece.

Top stitch around the dish shape.

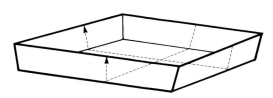

Measure width and length of dish, plus the sides.

5 Machine-stitch the outer edge allowing $\frac{1}{2}$in (1.25cm) seam allowance, and leaving a small turning gap. Turn through, press and slipstitch the opening.

6 Top-stitch $\frac{1}{2}$in (1.25cm) from the outer edge. Try the dish for size and lightly

mark the base area and then top-stitch around the dish shape to finish.

7 Sit the dish in the centre and draw up the sides. Tie the corner strips together to form a loose cozy coat which will keep your casserole warm.

Cherry pie pot holder

This decorative pot holder will protect your hands from hot dishes and the pie crust top-stitching will ensure it holds its shape even after repeated laundering.

Materials
2 × 11in (25cm) squares of cotton chintz and thermal lining
Remnants of red cotton and iron-on interfacing

Making the holder
1 Cut 2 circles of main fabric and 2 circles of heat-resistant thermal lining approximately 9in (23cm) in diameter (using a dinner plate as a template). Cut a strip for the hanging loop 6 × 1½in (15 × 4cm).

2 Make the cherry filling and appliqué cherries from a remnant of red cotton. Cut a triangular wedge 4½in (11cm) high × 4in (10cm) wide and two cherries, using a wine glass base as a template. Bond the cherry motifs to the right side of one main piece, positioning them just above the centre. Appliqué in position, adding white satin stitch highlights and green stems.

3 Prepare the pie filling wedge by interfacing the wrong side of the red triangle of fabric. On the right side draw the cherries using a small coin for size. Machine-stitch with black thread, adding white satin stitch highlights as desired.

4 Cut the wedge shape from the appliquéd circle of main fabric, 3½in (9.5cm) high × 2½in (6cm) wide allowing ½in (1cm) seam allowance. Machine-stitch the cherry filling in place, right sides together pivoting at top point. Neaten seams and clip close to the point before pressing the seams towards pie.

5 Fold the loop strip in half lengthways with right sides facing. Tuck the raw

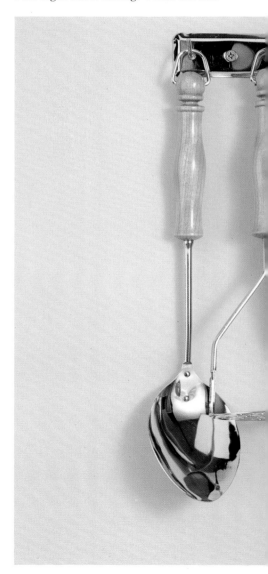

30

edges to the inside by ½in (1.25cm), machine-stitch close to the edge and then press.

6 Add the 2 circles of thermal lining to the wrong side of the appliquéd piece. Pin both ends of the loop to the top right side of the pot holder, matching raw edges. Pin the remaining circle of main fabric to the front, right sides together, sandwiching the loop.

7 Machine-stitch through all layers,

leaving a small 2in (5cm) turning gap. Neaten the seam allowance but leave it untrimmed.

8 Turn the pot holder through and slipstitch the opening. Press. Top-stitch two rows of machine-stitching, around the pie crust, approximately ¾in (2cm) from the edge. Finish with short diagonal lines of stitching at regular intervals around the edge.

Bread basket warmer

Keep breakfast rolls and croissants warm in this cheerful warmer. The simple square design has bound edges with ties that form snug pockets in which to tuck the rolls and pastries.

Materials
Fabric remnant 17 × 34in (43 × 86cm)
Iron-on interfacing 17in (43cm) square
3yd (2.80m) bias binding

Making the warmer
1 Cut two 17in (43cm) squares from the fabric. Apply the interfacing to the wrong side of one fabric square, then pin the two fabric squares together with wrong sides together, sandwiching the interfacing.

2 Open out and pin the bias binding around the edges of the joined squares. Machine-stitch in place before folding back over to the other side, encasing the raw edges. Pin in place.

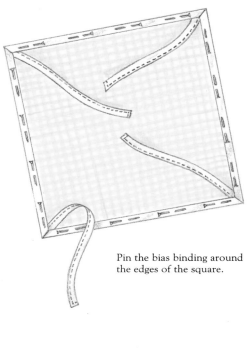

Pin the bias binding around the edges of the square.

3 Cut the remaining length of bias binding into four equal lengths for the ties. Treating each tie in the same manner, fold under approximately ¼in (6mm) inside one end and then sew the end and side edges together. Pin the raw, unstitched end of each tie to a corner of the warmer, tucking the raw edges under the previously pinned bias binding.

4 Once the ties are in place, top-stitch the bias binding edging close to the edge.

5 To use the bread basket warmer, fold the four corners to the centre and press. Tie the diagonally opposite corner ties together in the centre.

Fold the four corners to the centre, over the bread.

32

THREE

Small Talk

35

Playmat

Brighten up the playroom with this cheerful playmat. Comfortably padded, baby will enjoy hours of fun, while learning to identify the animals and toys.

Materials

2 × 11in (28cm) squares in each of red, blue and yellow cotton
½yd (50cm) of printed cotton for centre square and edging
33in (84cm) square of 8oz (200g) wadding
33in (84cm) square of calico (for backing)
11in (28cm) square of ready-printed quilting interfacing
10in (25cm) squares of Funtex (washable felt) in black, red, yellow, green, blue, orange, white and tan
2 squeakers
2 safety bells
Ribbon remnants
2 moving safety eyes, 1 black safety eye
Fabric paint
Bondaweb (iron-on webbing)

Making the playmat

1 First scale up the motif patterns using dressmaker's graph paper. Cut out the motifs from the washable felt, following the pattern provided. Make a small pocket for each of the two squeakers, using a fabric scrap. Sew one to the centre back of the clown's head and the other to the centre back of the duck.

2 Bond a motif to the right side of each of the coloured squares. Using fabric paint, add the letters, numbers and features to the blackboard, clock face and flower head. At the same time add the ribbon easel and flower stem, tucking the ribbon ends under the felt as you go.

3 Thread each bell on a small length of ribbon and pin in place. Machine-stitch using zigzag stitch around each of the motifs to secure firmly, catching the bell ribbon ends securely in the stitching on both the cat and flower head. Use matching or contrasting threads to define limbs and features as desired.

4 Add safety eyes to the clown face and duck. Then machine-stitch the decorative ribbon trims to the duck panel, easel, flower, clock and the hot air balloon. Finally, finish the dog with a hand-embroidered tongue. The cat has embroidered eyes and nose, with long stitches for the whiskers whilst the balloon is finished with cross stitches.

5 Cut an 11in (28cm) square of printed cotton for the centre panel. Interface and quilt the centre panel. With right sides together, join the panels in strips of three, with the quilted panel between the two blue panels. Join the three panel strips together to form a square, again keeping the quilted panel in the centre.

6 Pin the square of wadding to the wrong side of the joined panels and then add the calico backing, sandwiching the wadding. Machine-stitch all layers together around the outer edge. Trim seam to ½in (1.25cm).

7 Cut the remaining printed cotton into 1½in (4cm) wide bias strips until there are enough strips to make one long strip approximately 132in (3.4m) long. Sew the strips together end to end and with the panelled side facing and right sides together, pin and stitch the strip of printed cotton around the playmat's edge.

8 Fold the edging over to the back of the playmat, encasing the raw edges. Fold under ½in (1.25cm) and pin in place. Finally hand sew to the calico back.

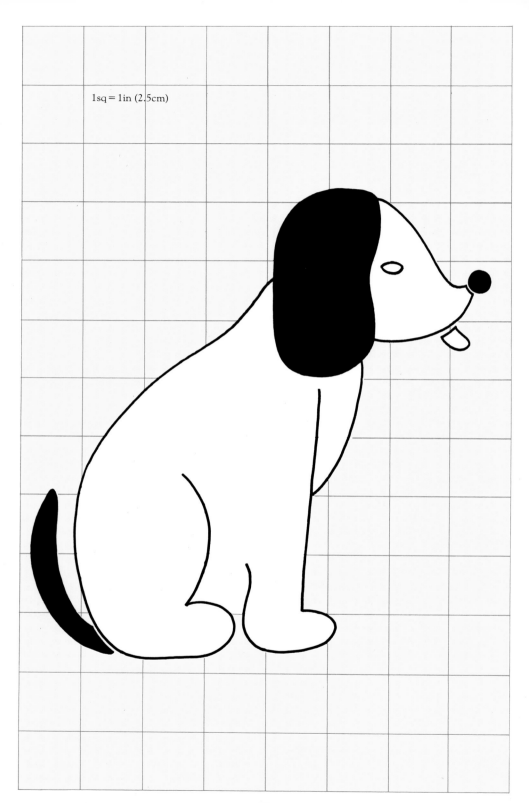

1sq = 1in (2.5cm)

1sq = 1in (2.5cm)

ABCDE
2+2=4

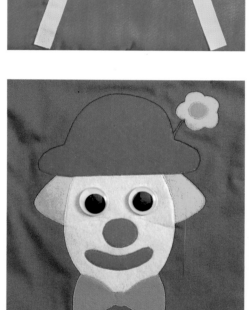

1sq = 1in (2.5cm)

1sq = 1in (2.5cm)

1sq = 1in (2.5cm)

1sq = 1in (2.5cm)

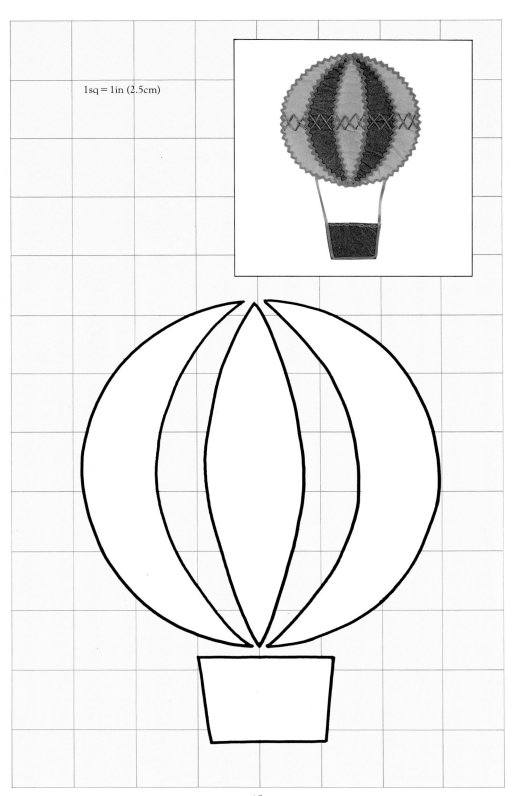

1sq = 1in (2.5cm)

Tiny teacher doll

This colourful and cuddly doll is not only fun to play with it also helps tiny tots learn about buttons, bows, poppers and plaits. Such a happy doll will be adored by children.

Materials
½yd (50cm) of jersey tubing
Fabric and Funtex or felt remnants
1 bag of polyester stuffing
1 (25g) DK knitting wool
1yd (90cm) bias binding
Narrow elastic for skirt
Narrow ribbon for shoe laces and plaits
2 buttons
3 poppers

Making the doll
1 Using the jersey tubing and the pattern provided, cut the front and back for the doll. Working with one body piece, form the nose by gather-stitching a circle, the size of a small coin, in the centre of the head. Lightly stuff the gathered circle. Then, with the right sides together, stitch the back to the front of doll, leaving a turning gap at the top of the head. Clip the seam allowance at the corners and curves and then turn to right side.

2 Stuff with polyester stuffing through the head opening, pushing down into each leg first. Once the foot is filled, hand sew through both layers of the leg to form the ankle joint. Repeat up the legs, adding knee joints and thighs. Continue stuffing the arms and body, adding joints for hands, elbows, shoulders and neck, working up to the head. Stuff firmly, shaping as you go. Slipstitch opening closed.

3 Add the hair using DK wool. Cut the wool into strands approximately 18in (46cm) long. Starting at the front, lay the strands across the head and sew in place at the centre. Continue down the back of the head to the neck, covering the scalp.

4 Trim the first few strands at the front of the head to form the fringe. Then catch stitch the hair to either side of the head at ear level. Plait as required, finishing with a bow. Embroider facial features using small back-stitches and colours to suit.

5 To make the socks, cut two rectangles of fabric 5 × 3in (13 × 8cm). Fold in half and stitch down the side seams, shaping the toe end with a gentle curve. Hem the top edges. Turn through and press.

6 Cut two shoes from Funtex or felt, following the pattern provided. Fold in half and sew the sides together. Turn through and then cut down the centre front. Snip small eyelets on either side of the opening for the ribbon laces.

7 The skirt is made from a rectangle of fabric 6 × 23in (15 × 53cm). Fold in half, with right sides together and stitch the centre back seam. Turn the top raw edge under 1½in (4cm), then turn edge under again, and stitch close to the turned edge. Stitch again close to the top of the skirt to form the casing for the elastic. Thread the elastic through the casing and slipstitch the opening. Finish with a machine-stitched hem.

8 To make the jacket and top, cut the pattern pieces from fabric remnants. Cut the jacket back and top front on the fold as shown. With fabric still folded, cut the jacket fronts and top backs. Sew the top fronts to the back at the shoulders and side seams. Sew a narrow hem at the armholes, neck edge and lower edge. Turn the centre front edges under ½in

(1.25cm) twice and machine-stitch. Finish with colourful poppers.

9 Sew the jacket fronts to the back at the shoulders and arms. Sew underarm and side seam in one go. Working from the inside, pin and stitch bias binding around the neck, front edges and hem. Fold binding over to the right side and

machine-stitch again, encasing raw edges. Repeat for the sleeve ends.

10. Interface the inside front edge of the left jacket front, then make two machine buttonholes, the size to suit the buttons. Finally, sew buttons on the right jacket front.

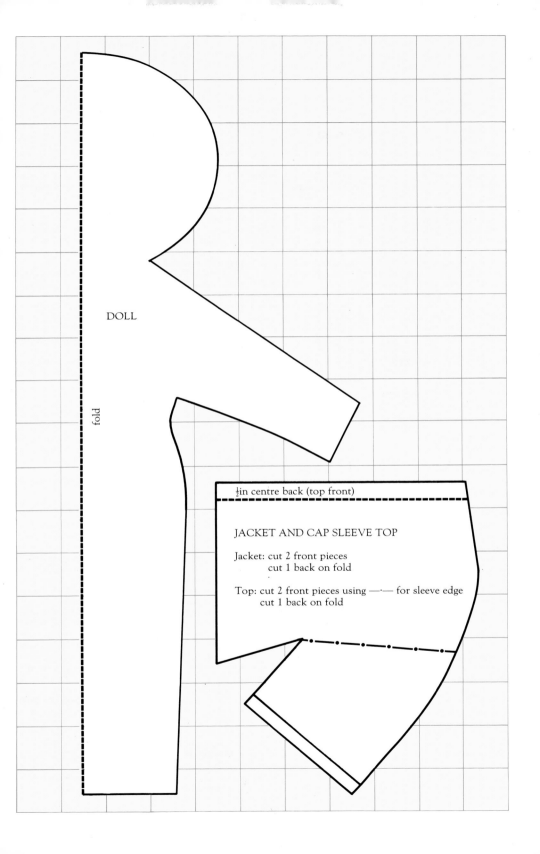

DOLL

fold

½in centre back (top front)

JACKET AND CAP SLEEVE TOP

Jacket: cut 2 front pieces
        cut 1 back on fold

Top: cut 2 front pieces using —·— for sleeve edge
     cut 1 back on fold

Colourful cot safe

Protect baby's head with this colourful bumper securely tied in place. The pretty design is enhanced by quilted overlapping circles and edged with striking red piping.

Materials
2½yd (2m) of 36in (90cm) wide fabric
3yd (2.70m) piping
72 × 14in (184 × 36cm) of 8oz (200g)
  wadding

Making the bumper
1 Cut 2 pieces of fabric 72 × 14in (184 × 36cm). Pin one length of fabric into three equal sections. Working on the right side of this piece, draw three overlapping circles on each third (using a small plate or bowl as a template). Pin the wadding to the wrong side and machine-stitch over the circles for a decorative quilted effect.

2 Attach the piping to the top and side edges, with raw edges of fabric and piping tape matching. At the corners, snip the piping tape to help smooth it around the curve. Machine-stitch close to piping.

3 Cut 16 tie strips, each 13 × 6in (33 × 15cm). Fold in half lengthways and machine-stitch across one end and up the side. Trim seam allowances to ¼in (6mm) turn through and press. Pin the ties in pairs to the right side of the quilted bumper piece placing them at the top and bottom of each side edge and all four corners, matching raw edges. Machine-stitch in position.

4 To add the back piece of the bumper, pin it with right sides together to the front quilted side, encasing piping and ties. With wadding uppermost, machine-stitch using the previous piping stitchline as guide and pivoting at the corners. Stitch around the edge, leaving a 12in (31cm) turning gap. Neaten seam allowance and turn through. Slipstitch the remaining opening.

5 Finally machine-stitch from top to bottom at the corners to help the bumper fold neatly into position.

Finished size of section

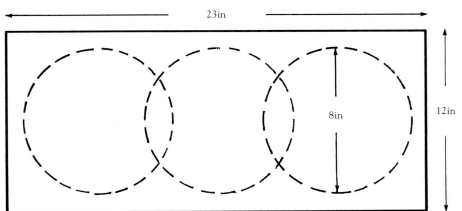

Clown appliqué cot quilt

This cot-size quilt brings all the fun of the fair, every night. The strong primary colours used for the clown motif will certainly appeal to tiny tots and brighten baby's room.

Materials

1⅛yd (1m) of 54in (140cm) wide white cotton sateen
1⅛yd (1m) of printed cotton sheeting for back
40 × 48in (102 × 122cm) of 8oz (200g) wadding
Fabric remnants and bias binding remnant for the clown motif
Bondaweb

Making the quilt

1 For the quilt, cut the front and back to measure 40 × 48in (102 × 122cm). Scale up the clown motif pattern and cut out from the fabric remnants, using the pattern pieces shown. Then, using a cup for a template, draw three circular balloons.

2 Bond the clown motif to the right side of the centre front quilt piece using Bondaweb, overlapping edges where pieces join. Press firmly in position and with a small zigzag stitch or satin stitch, appliqué the clown in place. Appliqué the balloons in the same manner, using matching thread for each appliquéd section. Finish the motif with bias binding down the centre front and satin stitch balloon strings.

3 Cut the wadding to the same size as the quilt and pin to the wrong side of the quilt back. Quilt in place to hold. Add the appliquéd front piece to the back with right sides together. Machine-stitch through all thicknesses approximately 1in (2.5cm) from the edge, leaving a turning opening in the bottom edge.

4 Trim the seam allowance to ½in (1.25cm), press, turn through and press again. Slipstitch the opening and then with the front facing uppermost, finish with a row of top-stitching all around the quilt, approximately 1in (2.5cm) from the outer edge.

Face pattern   1sq = 1in (2.5cm)

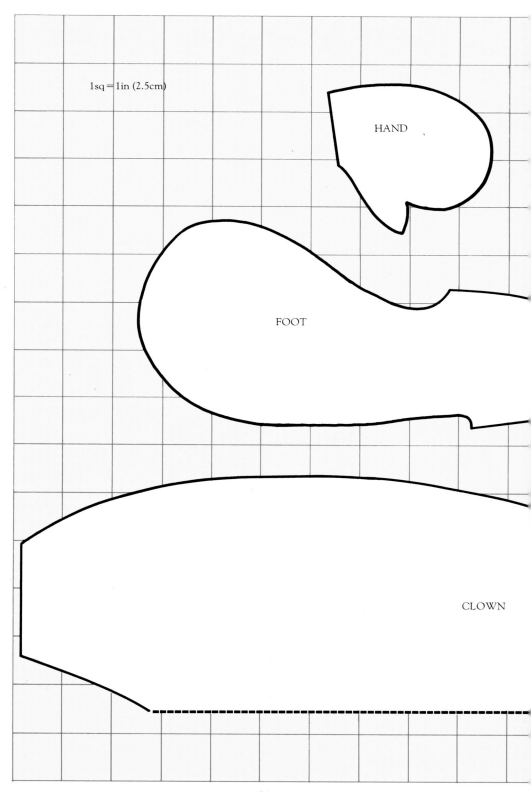

1sq = 1in (2.5cm)

HAND

FOOT

CLOWN

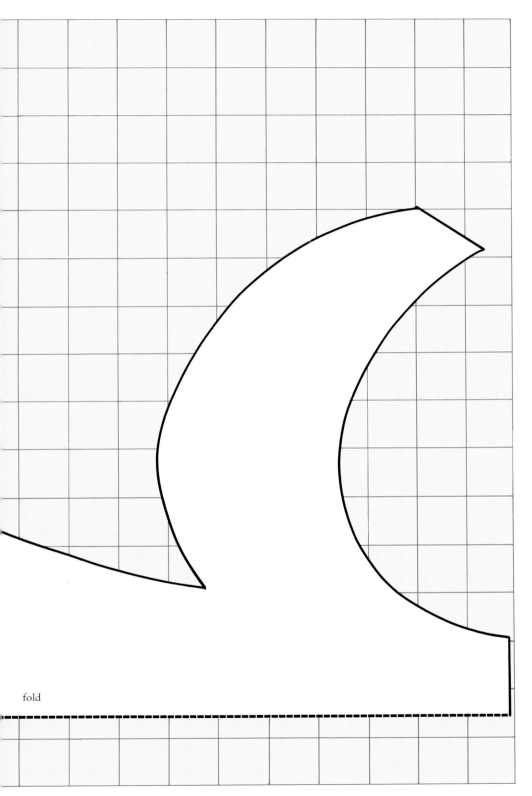

fold

FOUR

Al Fresco

Garden chair cushions

This stylish patio set of seat cushions will entice your guests to linger longer. Covered in reversible polka dot and spot, they can be turned to mix and match.

Materials

1½yd (1.40m) of 36in (90cm) wide polka dot cotton or chintz
1½yd (1.40m) of 36in (90cm) wide spot cotton or chintz
3yd (2.70m) of 4oz (100g) wadding
1⅜yd (1.30m) of 1in (2.5cm) wide elastic
4in (10cm) of 1in (2.5cm) wide Velcro
4 poppers

Making the cushions

1 Cut a pattern piece for the back and seat cushions, the back to measure 10in (25cm) × 12½in (32cm) and the seat to measure 15in (38cm) × 13½in (34cm). Round off each of the four corners.

2 Fold the polka dot fabric in half and cut out 4 seat pieces and 4 back pieces. With fabric still folded cut out 4 back straps, tabs and loops as follows: 4 straps – 3 × 18in (8 × 46cm); 4 tabs – 3 × 1½in (8 × 4cm); 4 loops – 3 × 12½in (8 × 32cm).

3 Fold the spot fabric in half and cut out the remaining 4 back and seat pieces. Using the same pattern pieces, cut out 2 wadding pieces for each back and seat cushion. Cut the elastic into 4 even pieces.

4 For each seat cushion pin a polka dot to a spot piece, right sides together. Add two wadding pieces sandwiching the spotted fabrics in between. Machine-stitch around the edges through all thicknesses, leaving a turning gap in one edge. Trim the seam allowance and turn through. Slipstitch the opening. Press carefully.

5 Make each elasticated strap by folding the strap in half lengthways, stitch the side seam and refold to the middle. Insert the elastic, gathering the fabric to fit. Turn raw edges of one end to the right side of the strap and pin in place, then cover with a 1in (2.5cm) strip of Velcro, machine-stitched in place through all thicknesses. Pin the other end of the strap, with underside of strap facing the right side of a back piece, approximately 5in (13cm) from the top edge.

6 Make the short tab in the same manner as the strap, stitching the Velcro to the underside of the tab (over the seam). Pin to the opposite side of the back section, again with the underside of the tab facing the right side of the back and matching raw edges.

The elasticated strap passes through the vertical loop.

7 Make the top loop by folding it in half lengthways and stitching the side seam and one end. Turn through and press. Pin the unstitched end to the right side of the back at the centre top edge.

8 Pin the remaining back in place, with right sides together, sandwiching the strap, loop and tabs. Add the two layers of wadding, one either side, again

sandwiching the fabrics. Stitch around edges leaving a turning gap. Trim seams and turn through. Slipstitch opening.

9 Try the back cushions on the chair backs adjusting the loop to the length required. Finish the loop with a popper to hold in place and so the cushions are easily removed or turned over when required.

Fragrant flower picnic mat

Enjoy balmy summer days and lunch al fresco with this colourful floral picnic mat. Each petal provides a place setting and the floral theme is further enhanced by the ladybird motif!

Materials
1yd (90cm) pale pink cotton poplin
1yd (90cm) rose pink cotton poplin
⅜yd (40cm) green cotton
⅜yd (40cm) yellow cotton
Iron-on interfacing
2 ladybird motifs

Making the mat
1 Using the graph pattern, scale up and cut out 8 pale pink and 8 rose pink petals. Cut a further 8 pieces of iron-on interfacing and apply to four of each shade of petal.

2 Add a plain petal piece to each of the interfaced petal pieces with right sides together. Machine-stitch around the outer edge leaving the straight edge free. Trim seam close to the stitching, turn through and press.

3 Fold the green fabric in half lengthways and cut out 8 leaf pieces. Again interface four pieces before machine-stitching them to the four plain pieces, right sides together. Trim the seam allowance, turn through and press. Slipstitch the opening. Then top-stitch the leaf veins in a contrasting colour.

4 Layer the pink petals evenly in a circle, pin in place, leaving a hole in the centre. Add the leaves between every second petal and pin in place. Top-stitch around the outer edge of the petals and leaves, stitching through all thicknesses where applicable.

5 To add the centre of the flower cut 2 yellow 12in (30cm) diameter circles, using a dinner plate as a template. Interface both centre pieces and then turn the

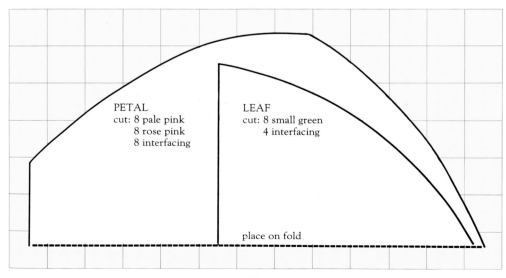

PETAL
cut: 8 pale pink
8 rose pink
8 interfacing

LEAF
cut: 8 small green
4 interfacing

place on fold

edges under approximately ½in (1cm), pressing in place as you go. Add random French knots for stamens to one centre piece and sew on the ladybird motifs as desired.

6 Working with the right side facing, position the decorated centre circle in place, covering the petal edges. Machine stitch around the edges in matching thread. Turn the picnic mat over, trim the petal ends close to the stitching and press seam towards centre.

7 Finish the underside by slipstitching the remaining yellow circle in place, covering the petal ends and the machine-stitching of the front centre piece.

Picnic cutlery caddy

This lightweight cutlery caddy holds six place settings plus condiments and napkins. The cord drawstring pulls together holding everything securely in place.

Materials
1yd (90cm) of 54in (140cm) wide
  lightweight cotton fabric
26in (66cm) of 36in (90cm) wide
  interfacing
1yd (90cm) of cord

Making the caddy
1 Cut one piece of fabric and interfacing for the caddy back 26 × 18in (66 × 46cm). Apply interfacing to the wrong side of the fabric and then fold the fabric in half with the right sides together. Machine-stitch the seam leaving a 4in (10cm) turning gap in the middle. Press the seam open and refold with the seam in the centre.

2 Stitch across the top, taking ½in (1.25cm) seam allowance. Starting at one edge, stitch 1in (2.5cm), leave ½in (1.25cm) gap for the drawstring, stitch remainder of seam to within 1½in (4cm) of the end; leave ½in (1.25cm) gap and then stitch to the end. Repeat across the bottom edge.

3 Turn through to the right side, press and slipstitch the opening. To form the casing, top-stitch ½in (1.25cm) from the top edge. Repeat across the bottom edge.

4 Cut the pocket piece 26 × 17½in (66 × 44cm). As with the back piece fold the fabric in half, short ends together. Stitch seam leaving a turning gap in the middle. Refold so that the seam is in the centre and stitch top and bottom seams. Turn through to the right side, press and slipstitch the opening.

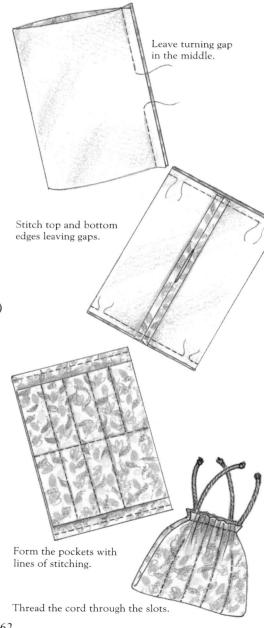

Leave turning gap in the middle.

Stitch top and bottom edges leaving gaps.

Form the pockets with lines of stitching.

Thread the cord through the slots.

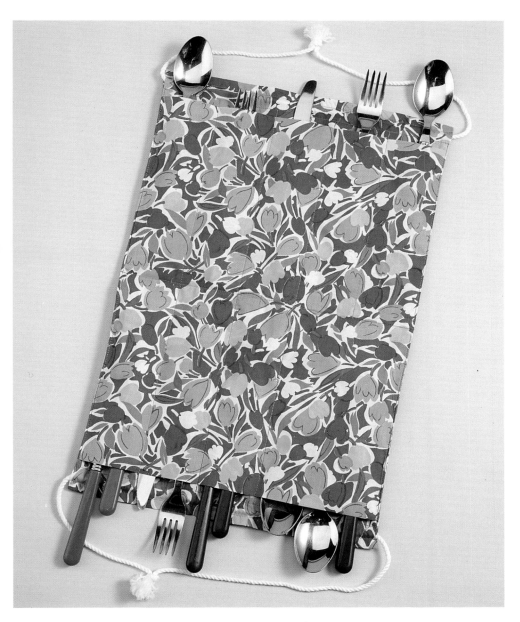

5 Pin the pocket to the back piece so that it is equal distance from the top and bottom edges. Stitch in place down the side edges and then horizontally across the centre. Form five pockets in the top half, each approx 2½in (6cm) wide for knives, forks, spoons and condiments. Then stitch three more pockets of 2½in (6cm) wide in the bottom half, leaving one end pocket 5in (12cm) wide for the napkins.

6 Cut the cord in half and thread one each through top and bottom slots, knotting each end. Fold the caddy up and draw the cord together to hold everything securely in place.

FIVE

Fun with Fabric

Drawstring beach bag

Bright and lightweight, this appliquéd beach bag will comfortably carry the necessary paraphernalia for a beach trip and the handy side pockets are ideal for sunglasses and tanning lotion.

Materials
½yd (50cm) of 45in (115cm) wide printed cotton
Heavyweight interfacing
Bondaweb remnant
2¼yd (2m) cord
D-ring
Cotton remnants for appliqué motif

Preparation
1 Cut the bag pieces from the cotton fabric as follows: main bag, 1 piece 12½ × 22in (32 × 56cm); pocket, 1 piece 12½ × 8in (32 × 21cm); cord carrier, 2½ × 3in (6 × 8cm); also cut one 9in (23cm) diameter circle in heavyweight interfacing and two in printed cotton.

2 Hem the top edge of the pocket, turning under ½in (1cm) twice to encase the raw edges. With right sides together, stitch the bottom of the pocket to one end of the main bag section. Then on the right side, stitch pocket sections from top hem to base at 6in (15cm) intervals.

3 Using the graph, scale up the picture of the windsurfer and cut pieces from cotton fabric remnants. Bond the board and each colour panel of the sail and place on the centre front of main bag section, overlapping the panels slightly. Satin stitch around all edges to secure in place before adding the satin stitch boom.

4 Stitch the back seam of the bag, with right sides together, leaving a 1in (2.5cm) opening, 3in (8cm) from the top. Press seam allowance open and neaten both edges.

5 Hem the top edge of the bag by folding over 2½in (6cm) and stitching 1in (2.5cm) from this fold. Turn the raw edge under ½in (1.25cm) and stitch again, catching the raw edge, to form the cord casing.

6 Fold the cord carrier piece in half lengthways, stitch sides together, turn through and press. Thread through the D-ring and then pin the carrier to the base of the bag over the back seam, matching the raw edges.

7 Trim the seam allowance from the circle of interfacing and then sandwich between the two fabric base circles. Turn the bag inside-out and pin to the bases with the cord carrier in place. Machine-stitch and neaten the seam allowance before turning bag through to the right side.

8 Finally thread the cord through the casing at the top of the bag and the D-ring at the base, knotting the ends together firmly.

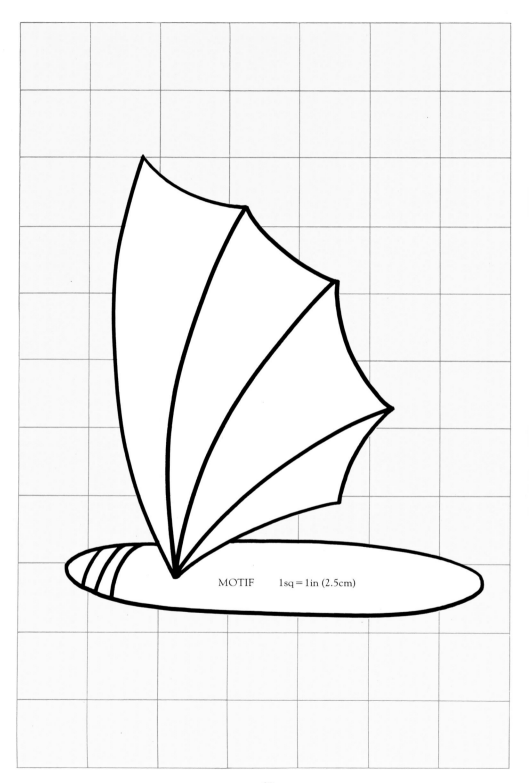

MOTIF   1sq = 1in (2.5cm)

Creative wall hanging

Enjoy hours of pleasure making this decorative wall hanging. Let your imagination run wild and fill the shelves with ornaments and books made from fabric remnants.

Materials

Background: 2yd (1.90m) of 36in (90cm) wide medium weight fabric

Wallpaper: 22in (56cm) square of printed cotton

Ornaments: fabric remnants

Shelves: 4⅜yd (4m) of ½in (1cm) wide brown grosgrain ribbon

1yd (90cm) of ½in (1cm) wide white grosgrain ribbon

Fans: ¾yd (70cm) each of two shades of ¼in (5mm) wide ribbon

Bondaweb and interfacing

Pattern for doll motif.

Making the hanging

1 Cut two pieces of the blue background each 30 × 37in (76 × 94cm). Interface both front and back background pieces. From the remaining blue fabric cut three hangers, each 5 × 10in (13 × 25cm). Cut the triangle of printed cotton, with two equal sides 22in (56cm) long, for the wallpaper.

2 Fold the hangers in half lengthways and sew side seam. Refold so that the seam is in the centre and press. Loop the hangers and pin evenly spaced to the right side, top edge of the back background, matching raw edges.

3 Place the wallpaper fabric on to the right side of the front background, pinning in place at the top side edges. Cut 5 stair triangles from a plain fabric remnant, each with two equal sides of 4in (10cm). Bond the stairs to the wallpaper, with the long edge of each stair on the inner edge of the wallpaper triangle. Zigzag stitch the stairs in place.

4 Next add the grosgrain ribbon shelving, with the top shelf placed 2in (5cm) from the top edge, the next four shelves at 5½in (14cm) intervals and the bottom shelf 7in (18cm) lower – approximately 3½in (9cm) from the bottom edge. Finish the shelving with two shelf dividers, one placed 11in (28cm) from the left side on the bottom shelf and the other 18in (46cm) from the left on the next shelf. Add the white grosgrain ribbon to cover the raw edges of the stairs.

5 Cut out the ornaments from fabric remnants. To make the doll, use the pattern provided; for the other ornaments use household objects as templates such as tea plates for the tea pots, bowl of flowers and fans – drawing the whole plate or part of it as appropriate. Cut different size rectangles for the books using a mix of ribbon and fabric remnants. Weave a wicker basket from the ribbon (see General Techniques) and cut flowers from floral fabric.

6 Appliqué the ornaments to the wall hanging using Bondaweb and satin stitch. Pad out one or two eggs and the flower bowl to add dimension. Trim the large eggs with decorative ribbon and add titles to some books. Make the fan spines from strips of narrow ribbon topped by lace trim. Add a hand embroidered flower to the top bowl and a little bow to the doll's shoe.

7 Once the decoration is complete, pin the front to the back, with right sides together, sandwiching the hangers. Machine-stitch around the outer edge, leaving a turning gap in the bottom edge. Turn through and press. Slipstitch the opening.

8 To make the lower pole casing fold the bottom end up 1½in (4cm). Machine-stitch close to the edge.

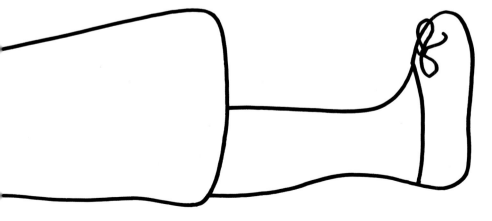

Tidy travel sewing caddy

Designed with travelling in mind, this petite sewing caddy is practical and pretty. Individual pockets hold the chosen haberdashery that will ensure you are prepared for any emergency.

Materials
Fabric remnant approx 11 × 36in (28 × 90cm)
Interfacing remnant approx 11 × 7in (28 × 18cm)
1yd (90cm) of 1in (2.5cm) wide satin bias binding
20in (51cm) of ¼in (6mm) wide ribbon for ties

Making the caddy
1 Cut the back, lining, pocket and needle threader strap from the main fabric as follows: back and lining each 11 × 6½in (28 × 17cm); pocket 11in (28cm) square; strap 2½ × 2in (6.5 × 5cm). Cut the interfacing to the same size as the back.

2 Attach the interfacing to the wrong side of the back piece, then quilt for a decorative finish. (Use a ready-printed interfacing with quilting guidelines for quick and easy quilting.)

3 Fold the strap section in half lengthways right sides together, and machine-stitch the long edge. Turn through and fold both ends under ¼in (6mm), press in place.

4 Fold the pocket section in half to measure 11 × 5½in (28 × 14cm) and then pin it to the lining section, matching side edges and raw edges at the bottom edge.

5 Machine-stitch the five individual pockets by stitching from top to bottom – the first line of stitching 3in (8cm) from the left edge and the remaining three, 2in (5cm) apart. Then pin the strap to the centre front of the second pocket, stitching in place at either side.

6 Pin the pocket and lining to the quilted back with wrong sides together and then round-off the corners, cutting through all layers. Fold the ribbon tie in half and with the quilted side of the backing uppermost, pin the folded edge to the right hand side seam allowance approximately 3½in (9cm) from the top corner.

7 Open out the satin binding and pin around the edges of the sewing caddy working from the quilted side. Stitch through all layers. Fold the binding over to the pocket side, encasing the raw edges, and slipstitch in place. Then fold down the top edge of the caddy to cover the pocket openings. Press with a damp cloth to give a good permanent crease.

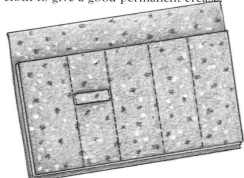

Machine stitch the five pockets.

8 Fill the pockets with haberdashery, slipping embroidery scissors in the wider end pocket, with buttons, needles, and pins in the remaining pockets. Make a thread carrier from a piece of card

$1\frac{1}{2} \times 5$in (4×13cm). Snip grooves down one side and wind on lengths of thread, securing the ends through the snipped grooves.

Perfectly pleated lampshade

Add the finishing touches to your room décor with this cleverly pleated coolie shade. To give a soft warm glow for romantic evenings, just add a pastel-coloured lining.

Materials
Main fabric: for the cover, measure a strut to determine the height of the shade and add 2in (5cm). Measure the circumference of the lower ring and multiply it by two to determine the total length of fabric required
2¼yd (2.10m) tape binding
½yd (50cm) lining
1yd (90cm) bias binding

Making the lampshade
1 First bind the frame by wrapping the tape tightly and evenly around the struts, top and bottom rings. Stitch the ends in place to prevent unravelling. This will then provide a surface on which to stitch the lining.

2 Line the inside of the frame by first cutting two rectangles of lining slightly larger than half-frame size. Lay each piece over the frame, pull taut and pin in place, pinning the two pieces together at the sides. Keeping the pins in the lining, carefully remove from the frame. Trim off excess fabric, leaving ½in (1.25cm) seam allowance at either side and approximately 1in (2.5cm) at top and bottom.

3 Machine-stitch the side seams and then neaten the top and bottom edges by turning under ½in (1.25cm). Fit the lining to the inside of the frame so that the seams are over the struts and the seam allowances face outwards. Pin around the top and bottom, stretching the fabric taut. Hand sew in place.

4 For the cover, cut the fabric to size – the height plus 1in (2.5cm) and the circumference doubled. Join pieces end to end if necessary to get the total length required. Turn the top and bottom edges under ½in (1.25cm) twice to neaten.

5 Pin one side edge of the cover to the top and bottom of one strut with ½in (1.25cm) overlapping top and bottom. Make tight pleats around the top of the shade, pinning each pleat through the top ring. Adjust the fullness as you go, finishing with the final pleat overlapping the first one.

6 Pin the lower end of the pleats to the bottom ring, again adjusting the fullness as you go. Once the pleats are pinned in place, oversew the cover to the frame, holding the fabric taut and removing the pins as you go. Trim the excess fabric away, close to the stitching at the top and bottom.

7 Hand sew the bias binding around the top and bottom of the lampshade, right sides facing, to cover the fabric edges. Fold the binding to the inside and catch stitch in place.

Sewing tip
When you have pinned the 2 pieces of lining fabric together at the sides of the frame (right sides facing), run a soft pencil or dressmaker's chalk pencil down the side struts, marking the fabric, before you take the lining off the frame. This will give you a guideline for stitching the side seams, and getting a perfect fit.

Quick-make shades

Pretty and lacy Make a cover for a plain, white lampshade using broderie anglaise fabric. Measure round the bottom of the lampshade. Cut fabric to three times the measurement by the depth of the shade plus 1in (2.5cm). Join the short ends. Press a ½in (1.25cm) to the right side on top and bottom edges. Stitch broderie anglaise edging round the bottom edge. Gather the top edge to fit the lampshade top ring. Thread ribbon through 1½in (4cm)-wide broderie anglaise eyelet edging. Sew the edging round the top of the cover. Then sew a ribbon bow with streamer ends at the front of the shade.

Mock pleating Bind the struts and rings of a drum-shaped shade. Catch the end of 1in (2.5cm)-wide taffeta feather-edged ribbon to the inside of the bottom ring. Bind the ribbon over the frame, overlapping the edges a little. Finish the ribbon end at the bottom ring, turning it under and catching it to the inside of the ring.

Sewing basket

Customizing a plain basket into an attractive sewing accessory makes a great gift idea. The lining has side pockets to hold threads and tapes, whilst a pin cushion and lid add the finishing touches.

Materials

12in (30cm) diameter basket requires:

$\frac{7}{8}$yd (80cm) of 36in (90cm) wide fabric

$\frac{1}{2}$ yard (50cm) of 36in (90cm) wide plain fabric

12 × 24in (31.5 × 61cm) of 4oz (100g) wadding

1yd (90cm) of narrow ribbon or elastic

2yd (1.90m) of 1$\frac{1}{2}$in (4cm) wide ribbon

1yd (90cm) of $\frac{1}{4}$in (5mm) elastic for pocket tops

Fabric-covered button

Felt scraps

Making the basket

1 To calculate the fabric required for any basket first measure around the outside, adding an extra 1$\frac{1}{2}$in (4cm) for ease and seam allowance. Then measure the height from base to rim, adding an extra 3in (8cm) for overlap, casing and seam allowances.

2 Cut the fabric to the required measurement for the lining. For the pockets cut another strip the same length × basket height plus 1in (2.5cm) seam allowance. Next cut the frill 3in (8cm) wide × the length and a half (joining strips if necessary to get the total length). From the plain fabric, cut 1 base section which should measure the actual size plus 1in (2.5cm) seam allowance. Cut 1 base from the wadding.

3 To make the pockets turn one long edge of the pocket piece under $\frac{3}{4}$in (2cm) turning the raw edge under again and stitch close to the turned edge to form an elastic casing. Before inserting elastic divide the total length into six equal sections for the pockets and press in creases. Then insert the $\frac{1}{4}$in (6mm) elastic, and pull up slightly. Pin the wrong side of the pocket piece to the right side of the lining, matching bottom edges. Machine-stitch together along the crease lines to form the pockets. Then stitch the short ends of both strips together to form a ring.

4 With right sides together, pin the lining pockets to the circular base, encasing and gathering the sides to fit evenly as you go. Add the wadding to the underside of the base and machine-stitch through all thickness. Cut two 'V' shapes in the top edge of the lining to go round the handles. Bind the raw edges with binding made from bias strips of the main fabric.

5 Cut the frill into two lengths and then fold each in half lengthways with wrong sides together. Gather the long edges and then pin and stitch to the right side of the lining 1$\frac{1}{2}$in (4cm) from the top edge. Turn the top edge over towards the frill to form hem and casing, tucking raw edges under $\frac{1}{2}$in (1.25cm) and encasing the raw edges of the frill at the same time.

6 Place the finished lining in the basket, with sides and frill folded over the rim. Insert the narrow ribbon or elastic through the slot under the frill to hold the lining in place.

7 To make the lid base, cut a lid-sized circle each in plain fabric, interfacing and wadding and pin together in that order. For the gathered lid cover, measure around the outer edge adding 1in (2.5cm) seam allowance multiplied by the radius

plus ½in (1.25cm). Cut a strip of main fabric to this length and stitch end to end to form a ring. Fold over ½in (1.25cm) on one edge and gather using large stitches. Pull up tightly and fasten off.

8 Pin the remaining raw edge, right side uppermost to the outer edge of the 3-layer lid base with the plain fabric on the bottom. Stitch ¼in (6mm) from the edge to hold the layers together. Neaten the edges with binding, made from strips of plain fabric cut on the bias and joined end to end. Finish the lid with a covered

button in the centre. Tie a ribbon bow to each handle to decorate the basket.

9 For the pin cushion, cut a saucer-size circle of plain fabric for the centre. Gather around the outer edges, pull up and stuff firmly with spare wadding. Cut a strip of patterned fabric 16 × 3½in (41 × 9cm). Stitch end to end to form a ring and fold in half lengthways wrong sides together. Turn raw edges to inside and press. Using large stitches gather edges and pull up tightly, fasten off. Stitch padded centre in place and add felt leaves.

Sweet dreams bedtime set

Add colour and comfort to your bedroom with this bedhead and matching holdall. Hung from a wooden pole, the bedhead is easily fitted to any bed. And the holdall tucks neatly under the mattress.

Materials for bedhead

2⅛yd (2m) of 60in (150cm) wide heavy
  cotton print or furnishing fabric
1⅝yd (1.50m) of 60in (150cm) wide calico
  for the backing
31 × 58in (79 × 147cm) of 1½in (4cm) thick
  foam cut to size

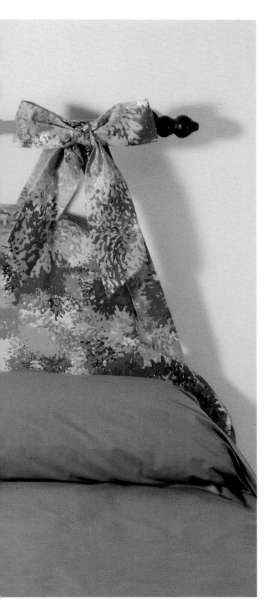

Materials for holdall

⅞yd (80cm) of 36in (90cm) wide heavy
  cotton OR
⅝yd (60cm) of 60in (150cm) wide heavy
  cotton
Interfacing for main pieces

Making the bedhead

1 Following the dimensions shown draw
and cut out a paper pattern for the
scallop. Fold the fabric as shown on the
layout. Then using the scallop pattern cut
5 pieces, matching one side edge of each
piece to the straight edge of the fabric as
shown. Cut 4 from the folded piece of
fabric and the fifth from a single layer.

2 Keeping the fabric folded as before,
mark out 2 hanging strips 18 × 5½in
(46 × 14cm) on the end of the folded
fabric so that each will measure 36in
(90cm) in length when unfolded.

3 Next mark out the bow strips starting
at one end of the single layer of fabric.
Each should measure 54 × 8in
(140 × 20cm). Finally, mark out and cut
the strips for the top gusset – cut 2
lengths of 2½in (6cm) wide fabric that
when joined end to end will measure a
total of 102in (258cm).

4 Cut the back sections and gusset from
the calico following the layout shown.
Again place one edge of each of the
scallop pieces along the straight grain.
Make the 54½in (138cm) long bottom
gusset from 2½in (6cm) wide strips of
calico joined end to end.

5 With the right sides together, sew one
front piece to the next along the straight
edges tapering at the pointed end. Repeat
until all five segments are joined together.
Join the calico pieces in the same manner.
Press all seams open.

6 Fold the hanging strips in half
lengthways, right sides together and sew
across one end and the long edge. Turn
through and press.

7 Pin the unstitched end of each hanging strip at an angle to the bedhead, right sides together. Position them close to the seams of the two end sections, angled so that the bedhead will hang evenly. Machine-stitch in place within the seam allowance.

8 Stitch the top gusset strips end to end to make one long piece 102in (258cm) long, then pin and machine-stitch it, right sides together, along the top edge of the bedhead front (over the hanging strips). Again with right sides together, stitch the calico back to the top gusset. Trim and clip seams then press.

9 Stitch the bottom gusset pieces together end to end to create one long piece 54½in (138cm) long. Keeping right sides together, pin and stitch the bottom gusset to the bottom edge of the bedhead, stitching the two gussets together at the sides. Continue stitching round part of the backing, leaving a large turning gap to insert the foam.

10 Turn through and press. Insert the foam and then hang the bedhead in place and pin remaining ends of the hanging strips to the calico back. Machine-stitch in place.

11 Finally, sew the mock bow ties by folding each in half lengthways, stitching along the side seam and diagonally across one end. Turn through and press, then neaten the remaining end. Tie the mock bow by forming a loose knot in the centre of each bow length; then, pull a loop from each end block through the knot. Tighten the knot. Hand sew to the hanging strips at the pole.

Making the holdall

1 Fold one short edge of the fabric towards the centre so that it measures 10½in (27cm) from the fold to the nearest selvedge. Mark out and cut 2 main pieces measuring 28½ × 10½in (72 × 27cm). From the remaining fabric cut one pocket 14 × 10½in (36 × 27cm), and the front

pocket 9 × 14½in (23 × 37cm) which includes an extra 4in (10cm) for four pleats. Interface the two main pieces.

2 Double hem the two pocket tops by turning under the raw edge twice and stitching ½in (1.25cm) from the edge. Then pleat the smallest (front) pocket at either side by folding the fabric to the wrong side approximately 1½in (4cm) from the side edge, and back again ½in (1.25cm) so that a ½in (1.25cm) seam allowance is left. Pin and press pleats in place.

3 Mark a placement line on the remaining, larger pocket approximately 4½in (11cm) from the right side edge. Mark a matching placement line on the front pocket, 5½in (14cm) from the right side edge. Then pin the pleated pocket over the larger pocket, with both right sides facing uppermost, matching side seams and placement lines.

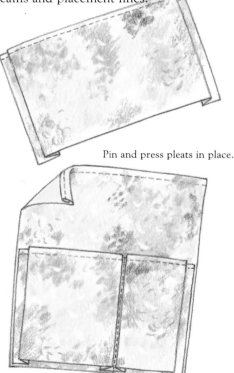

Pin and press pleats in place.

Stitch pockets together along placement lines.

4 Machine-stitch the pockets together along the placement lines from bottom edge to top hem. Make the remaining two pleats in the bottom edge of the front pocket by folding in the 1in (2.5cm) excess fabric either side of the line of stitching. Pin and press.

5 Pin the two pockets to the bottom edge of one main piece, again matching side and lower edges and with all right sides facing uppermost. Pin the remaining main piece over the rest with right sides together, sandwiching the pockets. Machine-stitch through all thicknesses along the bottom edge and up either side, leaving the top edge open. Stitch just ½in (1.25cm) from the edge so that the side pleats remain free.

6 Turn through to the right side and then turn under the remaining top raw edges of the main pieces. Top-stitch together and then press. Place the top half of the holdall under the mattress, letting the lower half hang down the side of the bed with the pockets facing outwards.

Position ties on the outer segments.

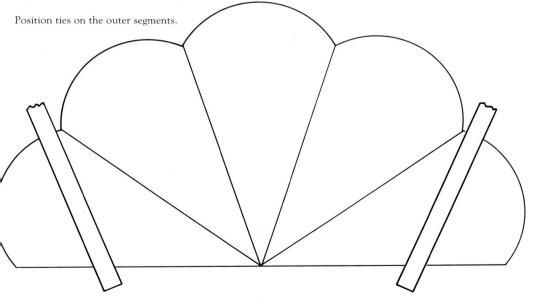

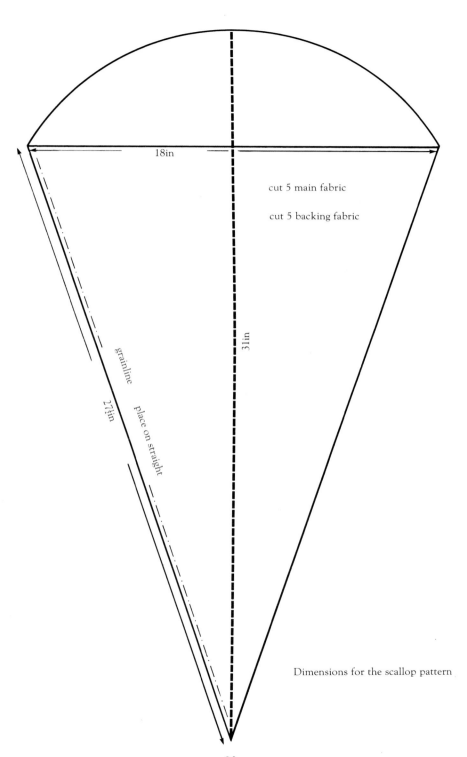

18in

cut 5 main fabric

cut 5 backing fabric

31in

grainline

27½in

place on straight

Dimensions for the scallop pattern

Fabric layout for bedhead cover

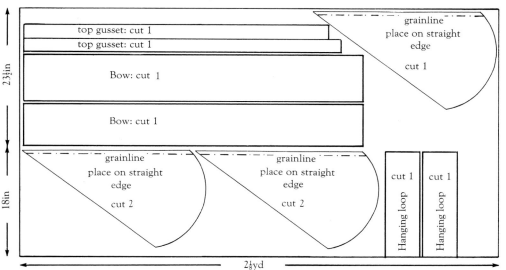

top gusset: cut 1
top gusset: cut 1

Bow: cut 1

Bow: cut 1

grainline
place on straight
edge

cut 1

grainline
place on straight
edge

cut 2

grainline
place on straight
edge

cut 2

cut 1

cut 1

Hanging loop

Hanging loop

23½in

18in

2⅛yd

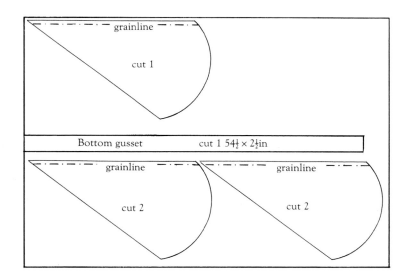

grainline

cut 1

Bottom gusset   cut 1 54½ × 2½in

grainline

cut 2

grainline

cut 2

Fabric layout for calico

SIX

Festive Favours

Holiday tablecloth

A festive Christmas table starts with the cloth and this parcel design has plenty of surprises in store with the elasticated pockets which make super hidey-holes for little gifts.

Materials

To fit 57 × 35in (145 × 89cm) table

2yd (1.90m) of red sheeting 90in (228cm) wide

1¼yd (1.50m) of 36in (90cm) wide green printed cotton

3½yd (3.20m) of 3in (8cm) wide satin ribbon

1⅜yd (1.20m) of ⅛in (3mm) wide elastic

Making the tablecloth

1 Hem around the red sheeting, turning raw edge under ¼in (6mm) twice and machine-stitching. Mitre each corner.

2 Using the green printed cotton, cut 2 parcel strips 44 × 10in (112 × 25cm) and stitch together to form one long strip of 88in (224cm). Cut a further 2 strips

33 × 10in (84 × 25cm) and again, stitch them together to form one long strip 66in (168cm).

3 Neaten the sides of each strip by turning raw edge under ½in (1.25cm). Turn each end under twice, to completely encase the raw edges. Machine-stitch across the end and approx 4¼in (11cm) up each side. Then gather-stitch across each end of both strips approx 4in (10cm) from the hem, and pull up so that the gathered material is 5½in (14cm) wide.

4 Position the parcel ties on the red cloth, crossing them at the centre. Machine-stitch down the side edges of both strips stopping at the gathered-stitching and thus leaving the remaining ends free. Cut the ribbon into 4 equal lengths, tie each one into a bow and add a large red bow at the gathered end of each parcel strip.

5 To make the surprise pockets fold the patterned fabric in half lengthways and cut 8 pocket shapes using the pattern. Hem the top edge and then turn under and press ½in (1.25cm) on the remaining edges. Cut a 6in (15cm) length of elastic for each pocket and stitch to the wrong side of the pocket, 1in (2.5cm) from the top hem, stretching the elastic to full width as you go.

6 Finally top stitch a pocket either side of the parcel strips, placing them level with the ribbon bows.

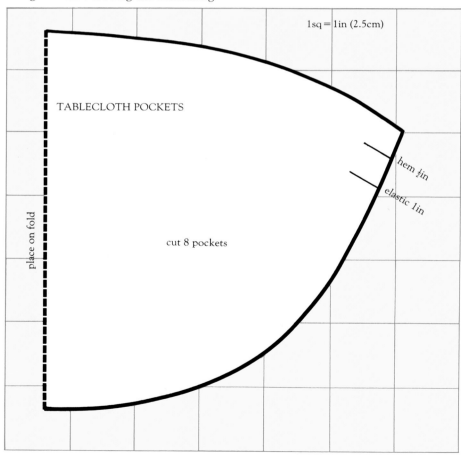

1sq = 1in (2.5cm)

TABLECLOTH POCKETS

hem ½in

elastic 1in

place on fold

cut 8 pockets

Santa Claus stocking

Hang this colourful Christmas stocking above the mantelpiece ready for Santa Claus to fill it with lots of surprises. The full boot shape ensures plenty of room to pack in presents.

Materials

To make 2 stockings:
20in (51cm) of 36in (90cm) wide red felt
White and green felt squares
Black fabric paint
Oddment of orange felt
DK wool oddments and polyester
  stuffing
1yd (90cm) of 1in (2.5cm) wide satin ribbon
Decorative fluffy balls and sequins

Making the stockings

1 Fold the ends of the felt to meet in the middle and using the graph pattern cut 2 stocking pieces for each stocking. For the snowman, fold a square of white felt in half and placing the pattern against the fold, cut one body and head piece. Cut holly from green felt.

2 Using the fabric paint, paint the coal black eyes and mouth on the face and leaf detail on the holly. Alternatively, embroider French knot eyes and use a running stitch for the mouth. Next, cut a triangle of orange felt for the carrot nose. Fold in half and stitch two sides together, lightly stuff and hand sew to the centre of the face.

3 Whilst the paint dries, knit the woolly hat and scarf. For the hat, cast on 10 stitches of DK yarn. Knit two rows, working in stocking stitch (stockinet stitch). Decrease at each end of the next and alternate rows until one stitch remains. Cast off. For the scarf, cast on 4 stitches and garter-stitch for 10 rows. Change colour if desired and knit another 10 rows. Change to a third colour for the next 20 rows, then repeat colours one and two for another 10 rows each. Add a ½in (1.25cm) fringe to each end.

4 Wrap the scarf around the snowman's neck and then pin him to one boot section approximately in the centre. Machine-stitch around the edges, stopping either side of the scarf and leaving an opening at the top. Stuff lightly, pushing the stuffing through the neck and rounding out his tummy. Slipstitch the opening and then hand sew the woolly hat at a jaunty angle.

5 Finish the snowman with a pompon for his hat and fluffy balls for his tummy held firmly in place by adhesive fabric paint/glue. Add a group of white fluffy snowballs, attached with fabric paint.

6 Position the holly leaves as desired on the boot and hand sew in place. Add groups of red sequin berries.

7 Fold the top of both boot sections under 1in (2.5cm) and stitch in place. Cut a 9in (23cm) length of satin ribbon for the hanging loop. Then pin the back to the front boot section with wrong sides together, pinning the ribbon loop in the seam allowance at the top edge. Using a contrasting coloured thread, machine-stitch around the boot edges, allowing ½in (1.25cm) seam allowance. Trim to ¼in (6mm) from the stitching.

8 Tie the remaining ribbon into a decorative bow for the top of the boot. Catch stitch in place at the centre front.

Trace-offs for leaf templates

90

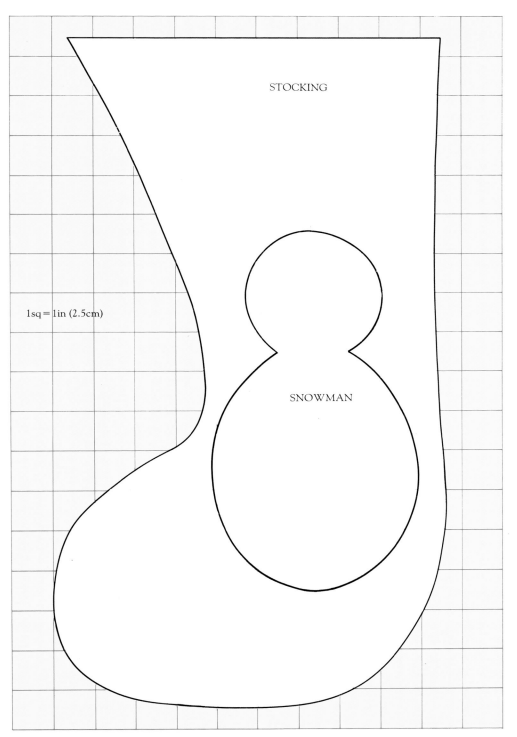

STOCKING

1sq = 1in (2.5cm)

SNOWMAN

Christmas tree skirt

Finish the tree decorations with these festive frills. A pretty, but practical tree skirt will hide unsightly pots or stands and provide a perfect backdrop for your pile of presents.

Materials
1yd (90cm) of 36in (90cm) printed cotton
½yd (50cm) of red cotton fabric
15½in (38.5cm) Velcro

Making the skirt
1 To cut the circle for the tree skirt, first fold the main fabric in quarters to form a square of four layers. Pin one end of a length of thread 17½in (45cm) long to the folded corner. Pivoting from this point mark off the radius of the skirt. Cut along this curved line through all layers.

2 With the fabric still folded in four, measure 1½in (4cm) from the folded corner down either side. Draw a line between the marked points. Cut along this line through all layers to make the top hole.

3 Open out circle of fabric and cut skirt from outside edge to centre hole along one of the creases. Narrow hem the centre hole, turning the edge under ¼in (6mm) twice to encase the raw edge. Turn the side edges under ½in (1.25cm) and press. Then pin strips of Velcro down both side edges and machine-stitch in place.

4 Cut the red cotton into 2½in (6cm) wide strips and then sew them end to end to form one long strip. Fold this in half lengthways with wrong sides together, and gather-stitch along the raw edges. Pull up so that the frill is approximately half its original length.

5 With right sides together, pin the gathered frill to the outside edge of the skirt. Adjust gathers as necessary and machine-stitch. Press the seam allowance towards the skirt and then edge-stitch to the skirt base.

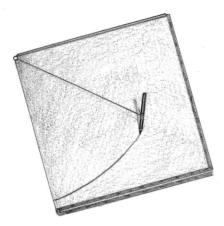

Fold the fabric into four
and mark off the radius of the skirt.

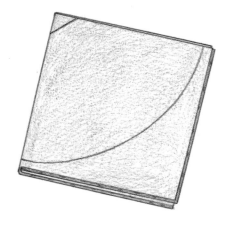

Draw a line across the folded corner.

Advent calendar

Countdown to Christmas with this easy-to-make advent calendar. A mixture of sweets and little gifts tied to the numbered rings ensures a special little surprise every day.

Materials
17 × 24½in (43 × 62cm) red felt
12¼ × 28½in (32 × 72cm) green felt
Brown felt square
Gold fabric paint
1½yd (1.40m) of ⅛in (3mm) wide ribbon for ties
24 brass curtain rings
1yd (1m) wide satin ribbon
20in (51cm) dowel ½in (1.25cm) diameter

Making the calendar
1 Take the red felt background and turn one end and both sides under ¾in (2cm) then top-stitch ½in (1.25cm) from the edge. Turn the remaining (top) edge under 1½in (4cm) and machine-stitch 1in (2.5cm) from edge to form casing for the dowel.

2 From the green felt cut 3 tree shapes as shown in the pattern. The first has a 12½in (32cm) base. The middle shape has an 11in (28cm) base whilst the top triangle has an 8½in (22cm) base with two equal sides 6½in (16cm).

3 Place the largest tree piece on the background 2½in (6cm) from the bottom edge. Then add the middle and top triangle overlapping each other so that the top of the tree is 2in (5cm) below the top edge of the background.

4 Before bonding and stitching in place, carefully stencil the numbers 1–24 in gold paint randomly scattered on all three tree sections. Then attach the tree shapes to

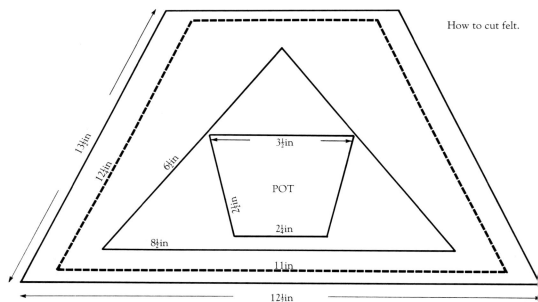

How to cut felt.

94

the background with Bondaweb and a large machine-stitch around the outer edges to secure.

5 Cut out and add the brown felt tree pot. Bond in place and then machine-stitch to secure.

6 Hand sew a brass curtain ring below each date from which to hang the daily surprises. It is now ready to add the individually wrapped gifts, tied in place with ribbon bows.

7 To hang the calendar, cut the wide ribbon into two halves, fold and stitch one end of each to form a loop. Insert the dowel through the top casing, adding a ribbon loop to either end. Then tie the remaining ribbon ends into a decorative bow.

Better Techniques

────────────── ❦ ──────────────

Sewing should be a pleasure, and so it can be if a few simple guidelines are followed. This chapter explains everything you need to know to successfully complete the wide range of projects featured. It also includes some general tips and techniques on sewing and how to avoid the most common pitfalls.

BASIC EQUIPMENT
Most households already have the basic tools required to begin sewing. However, it is a good idea to overhaul the sewing basket and ensure the equipment is in good useable condition.

Dressmaking shears
A good, sharp pair of dressmaking shears should only be used to cut fabric – not paper (and never use them in the kitchen!). They should have sharp blades with pointed tips, and shaped handles which will make cutting easier.

Embroidery scissors
A small pair of pointed embroidery scissors is extremely handy for trimming small areas, clipping seams and thread. The small size makes handling difficult areas much easier, with a greater control on the amount snipped or cut. Use them to avoid accidentally cutting through seams or clipping away more than is intended.

Paper scissors
A spare pair of scissors, that can be used for cutting out paper, patterns etc. Preferably choose a large pair so that

cutting out big pattern pieces does not become tedious. Always cut out patterns accurately along the cutting line, as an extra $\frac{1}{2}$in (1.25cm) multiplied by 2–3 seams could alter the overall effect and fit.

Quick clips
A small scissor with short blades and thumb control that is very useful for clipping small areas, tailor's tacks and thread ends.

Pinking shears
Very useful for cutting out craft fabrics, felt and card.

Rotary cutter
Ideal for cutting out patterns as the blade can be used alongside a straight edge, such as a ruler.

Scissor tuner
And finally, just in case you accidentally cut through a pin or otherwise damage your scissor blades, a scissor tuner is very handy. By running the faulty blade through the tuner, you can get rid of any burrs or snags that could catch on the fabric and cause unsightly pulls and tears.

Pins

There are many different types and lengths of pin, designed for various uses. For general use the glass/plastic-headed pins are preferable as they are easy to remove as you sew. They are also more easily found if accidently dropped! As with needles, pins will become blunt after repeated use so they should be replaced regularly.

Generally, it is advisable to pin at right angles to the seam so that the pins can be removed as you sew. However, when sewing fabric that marks very easily, such as suede, only pin within the seam allowance. It is also advisable to remove pins before pressing, otherwise you may press in a pin indentation that refuses to fade later.

Needles

Both sewing machine needles and hand sewing needles will become blunt after repeated use and should be replaced regularly. Needles are available in different sizes for different fabric thicknesses. Very fine point needles are used to sew fine fabrics, sheers and silks while a larger, heavier needle is used for coarser fabric. For sewing machines the choice is further extended to different *types* of needle for different fabric qualities. Ball-point needles are used for knitted/jersey fabrics – the rounded tip pushes the fibres apart rather than piercing them and thus prevents snags or runs. A jeans needle is extra tough for thick heavy fabric while a twin needle can stitch two rows at the same time.

Darning needle or bodkin

These are very useful for threading ribbon or elastic through casings.

Measuring aids

A good tape measure is essential for measuring fabric accurately. As a cloth tape measure can stretch with age and measurements may thus be inaccurate, a plastic-coated retractable measure is preferable, with both inches and centimetres to enable the choice of

Needle Chart

Fabric Type	Hand	Machine
Very light fabric: chiffon, silk, lace	9,10,11,12	9,11 (70,80)
Light fabric: silks, lawn, taffeta, voile	8	11 (80)
Medium light fabric: gingham, cotton, satin, wool crêpe	7,8	11,14 (80,90)
Medium fabric: flannel, velvet, pique, corduroy, linen	6,7	14 (90)
Medium heavy fabric: towelling, denim, tweed, felt, fleece, chintz, fake fur	6	14,16 (90,100)
Heavy fabric: wax-covered, ticking, corduroy, canvas, upholstery, fabrics, leather, suede	1,2,3	16,18 (100,110)

imperial or metric measurements.

A long ruler is also a good idea for drawing out diagrams and patterns and as a straight edge when marking out on fabric. Wooden yard sticks are available and are equally useful, particularly with hemming.

Tracing paper
Tracing paper is usually recommended for tracing same-size patterns or motifs but ordinary kitchen grease-proof paper will do just as well. Simply trace from the book and then transfer to the fabric, including any markings.

Dressmaker's carbon paper
Available in packs, dressmaker's carbon is used with tracing paper to transfer patterns to fabric. Place the paper carbon side down on the wrong side of the fabric and lay the traced pattern in position. Run a tracing wheel along the cutting lines to pick out the pattern. The carbon paper can be re-used many times.

Graph paper
When patterns are scaled down, they need to be transferred to graph paper in order to enlarge them to the correct size. Dressmaker's graph paper is available in various scales, thus it is necessary to use the paper that corresponds to the scale quoted on the drawing.

Chalk pencils/tailor's chalk
Tailor's chalk is used to mark placement lines, darts, pockets, points and other pattern markings on the fabric. A chalk pencil can be used to draw patterns directly on to the fabric. They are especially useful when no paper pattern is required – such as simple squares, rectangles or circles drawn round plates. Both chalk types should brush off easily; however, it is still advisable to make any markings on the wrong side of the fabric.

Quick unpick
A quick unpick is an extremely useful tool for quickly unpicking incorrect seams, saving a lot of time and

Chalk pencil

Quick unpick

frustration. To use, insert the longer edge point into the seam, with the beaded edge laid against the fabric. Push along gently, so that stitches will be cut by the sharp curve of metal at the end.

A quick unpick is also a great tool for slashing buttonholes. Place a pin at one end of the buttonhole to be slashed and then holding the fabric firmly in one hand, push the long edge of the quick unpick through at the other end of the buttonhole. With the beaded end resting on the stitching, push the quick unpick along until it reaches the pin.

Thread
The variety of thread types and colours now available can be overwhelming. As a general rule, however, use a thread made from the same fibres as the fabric – cotton with cotton, polyester with man-made, silk with silk. When in doubt, or when mixing fabric types, an all-round, very good general purpose thread is a polyester-covered cotton which has the give of cotton and durability of polyester.

To gauge the actual shade of the thread and ensure a perfect match, unreel a little and match with the fabric (in natural light). If the exact shade is not available, choose one that is slightly darker than the fabric.

Top-stitching thread
Top-stitching thread is thicker than ordinary threads and is ideal for machine-embroidery. However, top-stitching can be done just as effectively using ordinary thread.

Embroidery threads

Hand-embroided motifs, faces and highlights look better if stitched in embroidery threads. Available in skeins, there is a tremendous choice of colour and sheen. Although many skeins have six-strands these are generally split and used in two or three-strand thicknessess. In this book facial features have been embroidered and decorative detail added using three strands of embroidery thread. Other haberdashery items that are useful and time-saving include:

Point turner

A hard, usually plastic, ruler with a firm point. By pushing the point-turner into corners and angles, you can ensure a crisp, even point. Avoid using knitting needles or scissor points as there is a risk of pushing them through the stitching.

Fade-away pens

These are useful for marking stitching lines, darts, pleats or pocket placements. Even though the markings should fade, it is advisable to work on the wrong side of the fabric.

Turning loop

A thin metal rod with a catch hook on one end, a turning loop is ideal for turning through thin straps or ties. The hook is passed along the stitched tie to the end and hooked around the seam allowance before pulling back, turning the fabric to the right side.

Fastenings

There are many ways of fastening two pieces of fabric – from zips, buttons and poppers to lace and ribbons. The main fasteners used for the projects in this book are poppers, buttons and Velcro. The type of fastening to be used depends on the use of the item.

Closure tape – Velcro

Velcro consists of two strips, one with tiny hooks and one with a pile. When pressed together these intermesh and hold the two sides together.

Snaps/poppers

These are widely available in black, nickel or clear plastic in a range of sizes and weights.

Buttons

When attaching buttons, use three or four stitches with doubled thread or buttonhole twist thread. In addition, always wind the thread around the stitching between button and fabric two or three times which will then make it easier to fasten the button.

Buttonholes should be slightly longer than the button. Always interface fabric in which buttonholes are to be made for greater stability, before stitching the buttonhole. Without it, the close stitching can pucker and jam in the sewing machine.

Zip fasteners

Zips are the most common form of fastening on garments. Different weights, lengths and colours are available – the choice of which will depend on the item made. Generally, a lightweight fabric requires a lightweight, polyester zip. Heavier garments need stronger metal zips. The zip length should be $\frac{1}{2}$–1in (1.25–2.5cm) longer than the opening.

It is advisable to use a zipper foot when inserting zips in order to stitch close to the teeth. Always baste the zip in position and check for fit before machine-stitching in place.

Fabrics

Before you start any project, look through your scraps of fabric. You will probably find a remnant that you can use. When you are buying fabric for a dress or making a home-sewing project, it is a good idea to buy an extra half metre. This, together with any off-cuts, can often be put to good purpose, such as a set of matching accessories for a dressing table or some colourful items for the kitchen.

When selecting fabrics, remember that closely woven fabrics tend to fray less than loosely woven types. These fabrics are also easier to sew and generally give a good result. Make sure they have easy-care properties, so that they can be washed without the colours running and need little ironing.

Colours will be a personal choice, but when looking at a printed fabric, bear in mind the finished size of the project and avoid using large prints on small items. Most of the projects in this book will look best if they are made up in small sprig fabrics. The scale of checked and striped fabrics must be also noted; go for the small check ginghams rather than the larger versions whenever possible.

Interfacing

An interfacing is an extra layer added to the wrong side of the fabric. It is used to add body and to help with the drape. It can be another type of fabric that is compatible with the main fabric or it can be a branded interfacing. These are available in a variety of weights, either sew-in or iron-on and suitable for woven or knitted fabrics. The choice will depend on the effect required. As a general rule, however, the interfacing should be of a similar weight to the fabric and should also have the same laundering requirements.

When using iron-on interfacing, use a damp cloth and hot iron, pressing each area for approximately 10 seconds. Lift the iron, move to the next area and press again – do not push the iron along as it may stretch the interfacing or fabric which, in turn, will cause puckering. Always allow the fabric to dry and cool completely before continuing with the project. If handled too quickly, the interfacing may come unstuck.

Stuffing/filling

Polyester stuffing is preferable, particularly for toys, as it is washable. Do not be afraid of stuffing firmly, pushing into the corners and curves with a point turner or pencil. If inadequately stuffed, the item will very quickly lose its shape, so shape as you go, adjusting the stuffing accordingly.

Wadding (batting)

Wadding is the layer of fabric that is sandwiched between two other fabrics in quilting. Washable, polyester wadding comes in a range of different weights from light to an extra heavyweight (only used in upholstery). Use a lightweight wadding to give fabric extra body, and the medium and heavyweight versions for quilting, or when an extra layer for warmth is required.

Decorative trimmings

Small projects often look prettier with the addition of a decorative trim. Ribbons and braids come in most widths and the colour ranges are extensive so it is usually easy to find a good match. Besides plain ribbons in polyester satin, grosgrain, velvet and taffeta, there are printed ribbons, jacquard weaves and a variety of decoratively edged ribbons to be found. Attach narrow ribbons and braids by stitching them down the centre. With wider ribbons, machine-stitch down both edges, always stitching in the same direction to prevent puckering.

Sewing machine

Although a sewing machine is not essential it certainly speeds up sewing! Basic requirements include straight-stitch, zigzag, satin stitch and easy buttonholes, a choice of feet including a zipper foot and a choice of stitching speeds. Sewing machines range from basic models to high-tech computerized machines with endless stitch combinations. Bear in mind these when buying a machine:

1 Choose one that has the features you need now and some you might want in the future.
2 Look for good basic features: choice of automatic stitches, stitch speed regulator, simple buttonholes, easy foot control, variable needle position, good operator manual or video.
3 Try out the machine in the shop, testing on your own fabrics.
4. Ensure that there is a good after sales service.

TO BEGIN – PATTERN MAKING

It is advisable to make a pattern when two or more pieces of the same size are required. Patterns can be cut in paper, tissue paper or card – the choice will depend on how often they are to be used.

Cutting a pattern

Trace the pattern from the book using tracing paper and a felt pen. Add any notations such as *fold*, *cut 2*. The patterns in this book include a seam allowance of $\frac{1}{2}$in (1.25cm). If, however, seam allowances are not included, remember to add them to all sides of a pattern piece. Cut out the pattern pieces and lay them on the fabric, matching grainlines or fold as appropriate.

Graph patterns need to be transferred to the correct size by using scaled graph paper. Draw to scale by matching square to square and then, once completed, cut out and use in the same manner as a traced pattern.

The simplest patterns are made by drawing around existing objects. Household objects such as plates, cups and bowls make excellent templates.

Layout

Whenever possible, fold the fabric in half and cut through two layers at once. This not only saves time, it ensures corresponding right and left pieces are

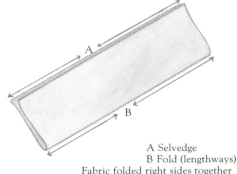

A Selvedge
B Fold (lengthways)
Fabric folded right sides together

accurately cut. Always fold fabric right sides together so that any markings are made on the wrong side.

Generally, fabric is folded lengthways. This means the fabric is folded so that the selvedges are together. If the instruction is to fold crossways, fold the fabric end to end, again right sides together.

If it is inappropriate to fold the fabric, or the instructions say to cut from a single layer, lay the pattern piece on the right side of the fabric. A pattern piece that needs two pieces cut should then be flipped over, face down, for the second piece in order to get a left and right piece.

Fabric grain

Following the grain line is extremely important when laying patterns and cutting out fabric. The grain line generally referred to is parallel to the selvedge – along the lengthways threads. The crossways grain is at right angles to the lengthways grain. If patterns are laid even slightly off-grain, the fabric pieces may ripple, pull or pucker when stitched, ruining the finished appearance.

Seam allowance

All the patterns in this book include a seam allowance of $\frac{1}{2}$in (1.25cm). Most new sewing machines have measured grooves in the footplate so that the seam allowance can be accurately maintained. If your machine does not have this guide, stick a strip of masking tape to the footplate as a guideline.

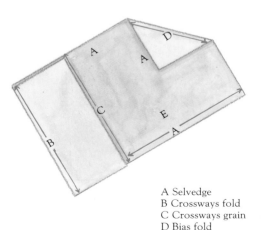

A Selvedge
B Crossways fold
C Crossways grain
D Bias fold
E Lengthways grain

Tailor's tacks

Darts, pocket placements and pleats need to be transferred from the pattern to the fabric. The traditional method uses tailor's tacks. These are large-looped stitches made at the placement points through both layers of the fabric before the pattern is removed.

Use a contrasting thread and make 3–4 large, loose stitches. Cut the threads carefully, remove the pattern and then gently pull the two fabric layers apart, cutting the threads between the layers as you go. Both layers will then have corresponding markings. Alternatively, use a chalk pencil, fade-away pen or dressmaker's carbon paper, again marking both fabric layers.

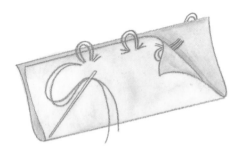

Tailor's tacks – large-looped stitches

Basting/tacking

When joining two pieces of fabric it is sometimes advisable to baste (tack) them together first. While straight seams can be pinned and machine-stitched without basting, trickier curved areas should be basted together. This will ensure that both layers are fed through the machine-stitched at the same pace, avoiding one layer creeping or stretching.

To baste (tack), knot one end of the thread and with a running-stitch, make ½in (1.25cm) long stitches along the stitching line. Use a contrasting thread that is clearly visible later. To remove, clip the knot and pull through. On long seams, it is advisable to clip and remove the basting thread at intervals.

STITCHING

Different stitching techniques can be used to make seams, attach motifs or as a decorative finish. The following are a few of the most common stitches and those used throughout this book.

Machine stitches
Straight stitch

The most common and standard stitch used to sew seams. First pin the fabric layers, right sides together, placing the pins at right angles to the fabric for easy removal. Then stitch, back-stitching at the begining and end of each seam. The stitches should be even in size and tension. If puckering occurs, increase the stitch length slightly. Always test on a scrap of fabric first.

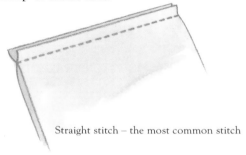

Straight stitch – the most common stitch

Zigzag stitch

This very versatile stitch is often used to neaten seam edges and as a decorative finish. Use a small zigzag stitch on lightweight fabrics and a larger stitch for the heavier fabrics. A zigzag stitch can also be used to sew seams on stretchy jersey. The finish will have more give and will be less likely to snap when stretched.

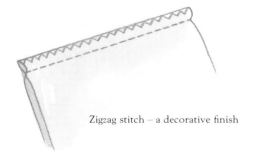

Zigzag stitch – a decorative finish

Gathering stitch

Large, loose stitches are used to gather fabrics for ruffles and frills. For long stretches of gathering, break off the thread at intervals which will be easier to gather than one long row. To gather, pull up each of the threads, adjusting fullness as you go.

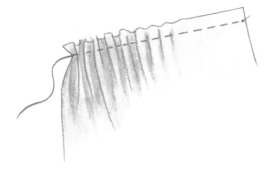

Stay stitch

Curved areas and areas that require extra handling should be stay-stitched prior to joining pieces. This is to prevent unwanted stretching. Simply stitch in the seam allowance, approximately $\frac{1}{8}$in (3mm) from the edge using a normal size stitch.

Satin stitch

A very close zigzag-stitch that looks like one continuous line. To make satin-stitch, adjust the width and length dials until the width is approx $\frac{1}{8}$in (3mm) and there is hardly any gap between stitches. A ball-point needle is preferable as it will suit most fabrics. To achieve a smoother satin-stitch slightly loosen the upper tension.

Top-stitching

Top-stitching is simply a term used to describe stitches on the top, outer side of a garment or item. Top-stitching can be in a contrasting or matching thread and it can be a simple straight stitch or a decorative stitch.

Always stitch with the right side uppermost, taking it slowly and carefully as, of course, the stitching will be visible. If two rows are stitched close together, try using a twin needle which stitches both lines at once. Use contrasting thread when you are confident of achieving a very straight even line of stitching. Finally, as top-stitching is purely decorative, it can be left out if preferred.

Hand stitches
Slipstitch

This is used to join 2 folded edges, such as a gap in a seam. Working from right to left, bring the needle out through the upper folded edge. Slip the needle through the lower folded edge for about $\frac{1}{4}$in (6mm). Pull the needle and thread through. Slip the needle through the upper folded edge for about $\frac{1}{4}$in (6mm). Pull through and continue through opposite folded edges.

Hemming stitch

Used for hems or when finishing the underside of a bound seam, simply take up a single thread from the garment fabric and then bring the needle up diagonally through the edge of the binding or hem allowance.

Blind stitch

Similar to hemming stitch and also often used to hem garments, a blind stitch is inconspicuous as it is hidden. This is achieved by rolling back the edge of the hem or facing about $\frac{1}{4}$in (6mm), picking up one thread from the hem, then picking up one thread from the garment diagonally below. Repeat from hem to garment, without pulling the stitches tight. Roll the edge down and press. No stitching should be visible.

Back-stitch

This is a strong stitch, useful for repairing seams and for hard-to-reach seams that can not be machined. On the right side the finished seam will look as if it is machine-stitched whilst the stitches on the underside will overlap and be twice as long.

With right sides together, bring the needle to the upperside along the seam line. Go back through to the underside approximately ⅛in (3mm) behind the first point, bringing the needle to the upperside again ⅛in (3mm) in front of the first point. Keep inserting the needle through the left side of the previous stitch and bringing it back up a stitch ahead.

Running stitch

As a very basic and quick stitch the running stitch is used for easing and gathering. Several stitches can be worked in one go, running the needle in and out of the fabric before pulling the thread through. Use large stitches for gathering and smaller stitches for easing.

Ease-stitch

Ease-stitch is formed by a running stitch and is used to stabilize and ease a fabric edge. It is used when a full or curved edge is to be joined to a straight edge. By ease-stitching the curved edge, you can ease the fullness into the straight edge.

Overhand/whipstitch

Basically the same stitch, they hold two edges together – an overhand or a whipstitch is particularly useful for adding lace edgings or ribbon trims. Insert the needle from back to front, up over the top and back through again. An overhand stitch is inserted at a diagonal angle and whipstitch is inserted from back to front at right angles to the fabric.

Embroidery stitches

There are literally hundreds of embroidery stitches to choose from when you are decorating fabrics. Here in the book are some of the most popular.

Straight stitch

These are often used on dolls' faces to indicate eyelashes and sometimes for attaching felt eyes. The stitches are worked in a six-point star. Bring the needle through at A, insert it at B and bring it through again at C.

Chain stitch

This is a simple yet effective decorative stitch. Bring the needle through at A and, with the thread below the needle, insert it beside A at B. The thread forms a loop. Bring the needle through at C, pull through gently, ready to start the next chain-stitch. To work a detached chain-stitch, from C work a tying-stitch over the loop.

French knots

A French knot is made by twisting the thread around the needle. First bring the needle through to the front of the work in the place that the knot is to be made. Holding the thread taut, wrap it around the needle three times. Insert the needle back through the work close to the point where it emerged until the knot remains on the fabric surface.

SEAMS AND SEAM FINISHES

In this book we have mainly used straight seams as the most common and easily created seams. A straight seam is formed by placing fabric layers, right sides together, matching raw edges and stitching along the stitching line – leaving ½in (1.25cm) seam allowance.

French seam

A French seam is ideal for sheer fabrics as it encloses all raw edges giving a very neat finish to both sides of the fabric. On the outside it looks just like an ordinary straight seam, inside is a neat tuck.

Pin the *wrong* sides together, and then sew ¼in (6mm) from the raw edges. Trim the seam allowance to within ⅛in (3mm) and press. Fold back along the seam so that the *right* sides are together. Machine-stitch along the stitching line, which is now ¼in (6mm) from the seamed edge. Press again.

Stretchy seams/sheer fabrics

When fabric has been cut on the bias or is a stretchy fabric, one of the fabric layers may tend to stretch when stitching. Similarly, very lightweight voile or sheer fabrics can pucker or jam in the machine. To prevent either problem arising, place a layer of tissue paper between the fabric and footplate. Stitch in the normal way, through both fabric and paper. Then tear the paper away.

Bias cut edges

Again use tissue paper under the seam to prevent uneven stretching. In addition, slightly stretch the fabric as you stitch so that the finished edge will not pucker. Before hemming garments with bias seams, hang overnight to allow them to stretch to their natural level.

SEAM FINISHES

The seam allowance should be neatened or finished, not just to give a neat appearance but also to prevent fraying and to help support the garment shape. The type of seam finish desired will depend on the use of the item and weight of the fabric.

For lightweight fabrics both the seam allowances can be folded to one side and treated as one. Again, either turn the raw edges of both to the inside and stitch together, or zigzag stitch over the edges. Another finish for lightweight seams is the self-bound seam. Trim one seam allowance to a scant ⅛in (3mm) and then turn the raw edge of the remaining seam allowance under and machine-stitch over the trimmed seam.

For mediumweight fabrics, each seam allowance should be treated separately. First press the seam open, then either turn the raw edge under ⅛in (3mm) on both sides and machine stitch – working in the same direction in which seam was sewn, or zigzag stitch over the edge of either side.

For heavyweight fabrics, such as unlined jackets or coats a bound edge is ideally suited. Open out the seam allowances and press. Then encase each raw edge in double fold bias binding and machine-stitch in place.

Seam allowances that will be encased can be graded or layered to avoid bulk. Cut the lower seam allowance to a scant ⅛in (3mm) and the next one slightly larger. This will also provide a smoother line.

SPECIAL EFFECTS
Appliqué

Appliqué is an attractive and simple way of adding motifs, colour and texture by attaching different fabrics to the base fabric. There are two popular ways in which to appliqué, the easier and quicker of these is the bonded method.

First cut the piece to be appliquéd according to the specific pattern. Add Bondaweb, a fusible adhesive with paper backing, to the wrong side of the appliqué. Peel the backing off and place on the right side of the main fabric, in the position required. If different pieces join together, overlap the edges by ⅛in (3mm) before pressing with a damp cloth to bond in place. Finish with a satin-stitch around the edges. Use a top thread that matches the appliqué and white bobbin thread.

Peel off the backing paper.

If the appliqué fabric or main fabric cannot be dampened and heavily pressed because of the texture, an alternative, dry method can be used. Cut a square around the appliqué, at least 1in (2.5cm) wider than the appliqué itself. With the right sides uppermost, pin in place. Using a small straight stitch, machine around the appliqué edge before trimming the excess fabric away from the appliqué square. Trim close to the stitching. Finish as before with a satin stitch border.

Quilting

The textured look of the quilting is created by stitching two or more layers of fabric together in a set design or pattern. For added thickness and in order to produce the traditional raised effect, the layers can include one of wadding, flannel or foam. An easy alternative is to use a special iron-on Quiltex interfacing. The lines of adhesive provided can then be used as quilting guidelines.

For a very special effect, quilt round the fabric design or part of it to emphasize specific design features. The following tips will ensure trouble-free quilting:

●Experiment on a sample of the fabric layers to be quilted to check tension.
●Baste all layers together around the edges and, if it is a large area, across the centre. This will prevent the layers shifting unevenly.
●Mark quilting lines on the right side of the fabric with a chalk pencil unless using ready-printed interfacing. If the quilting is to follow the fabric design, use that as your stitching guide.
●Quilt garment sections before joining them together as large areas of quilting can reduce the overall size of the fabric piece.

Ribbon weaving

A woven area of ribbon adds a decorative finish to cushions, pillow slips etc.

To weave ribbon first decide on the size of the area required and cut a piece of Bondaweb to that size. Cut the ribbon for the horizontal and vertical strands into equal lengths 1in (2.5cm) longer than the width and length of the piece to be woven. Anchor the Bondaweb to a padded surface or piece of card and then pin the top end of the vertical ribbon strips to the Bondaweb. Add the horizontal strips one at a time, weaving in and out of the vertical strips. Pin either side to hold in place. Once completed, press to bond and then turn the raw edges under and position the woven panel as required on the main fabric.

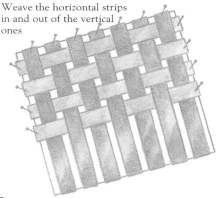

Weave the horizontal strips in and out of the vertical ones

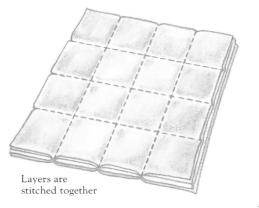

Layers are stitched together

ENGLISH/AMERICAN GLOSSARY

English	American
Bias binding	Bias strip
Cotton wool	Surgical cotton
Elastic bands	Rubber bands
Iron-on interfacing	Non-woven fusible interfacing
Polyester wadding	Polyester batting
Tacking	Basting

Knitting

Cast off	Bind off
Stocking-stitch	Stockinet-stitch

FINISHING TOUCHES

Piping: Piping is a strip of bias-cut fabric, folded and set into a seam for a decorative finish. For a harder-wearing finish, such as on cushions, the piping covers cord.

Piping cord comes in several thicknesses for different applications. To estimate the width of the covering fabric measure round the cord and then add twice ⅝in (15mm).

Bias strips: First, find the bias of the fabric. Fold over a corner of the fabric to meet the cut edge, the diagonal fold is the bias of the fabric. Cut through this fold. Use a rule and tailor's chalk to measure strips of the desired width from the diagonally cut edge.

Pin, baste and stitch strips together along the straight grain ends.

Place the cord centrally to the wrong side of the fabric and fold the strip round the cord. Baste closely against the cord. With a piping foot on the sewing machine, stitch down the strip close beside the cord.

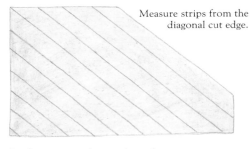

Measure strips from the diagonal cut edge.

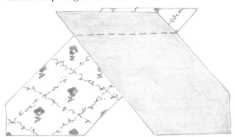

Stitch strips together on the ends.

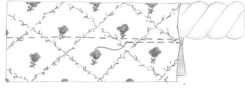

Stitch the fabric round the cord.

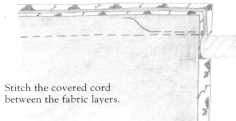

Stitch the covered cord between the fabric layers.

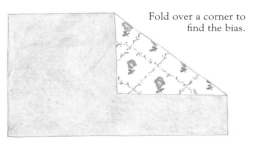

Fold over a corner to find the bias.

108

Inserting piping: Baste the prepared piping between two fabric layers, matching raw edges. Stitch on the seam line.

Joining piping: Start stitching ⅜in (9mm) from the end. When you come to the other end trim the cord to meet the first cord. Trim the fabric covering back to ½in (12.5mm). Butt the cords, dab a touch of fabric adhesive to the ends so that they stick together. Fold under the trimmed fabric edge ¼in (6mm). Wrap over the starting end of the piping. Continue stitching.

Frills

Single frill: Decide on the finished width of the frill and add ½in (12.5mm) for a doubled hem and ⅝in (15mm) for the seam allowance. To estimate the length, measure along the place to be frilled and double the measurement. (If the fabric is very thick, only allow one and a half times the measurement.) Turn a double ¼in (6mm) hem along the bottom edge. Press and machine-stitch.

Work 2 rows of gathering-stitches along the top edge either side of the seamline. (If the frill is very long, divide the frill into equal sections and gather each section in turn.) Pull the gathers up evenly to fit the main fabric. Pin, then baste the frill to the main fabric, working across the gathering-stitches to hold the frill in place. Stitch the frill in place.

Remove basting threads. If the ends need to be neatened, work a double hem to match the bottom hem before gathering.

When making up a continuous frill, such as for a cushion, pin and stitch the frill-strip short ends together into a ring before gathering.

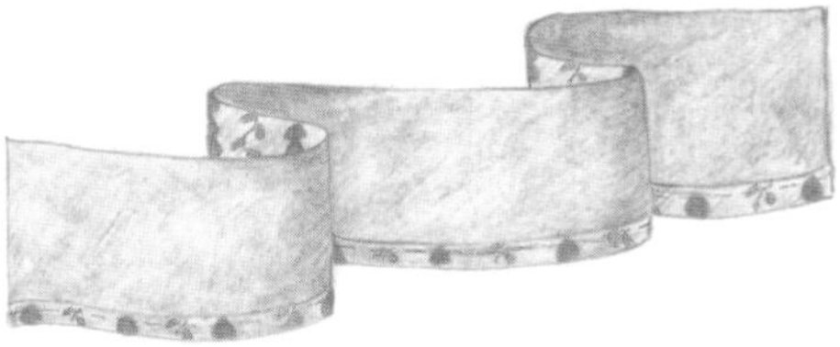

Turn and stitch a double hem on a single frill.

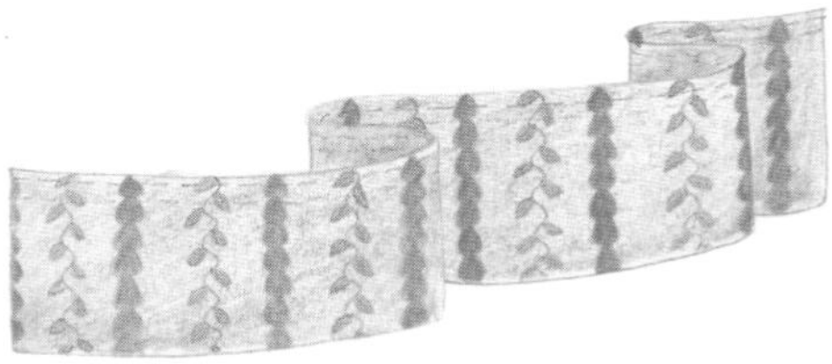

Work 2 rows of gathering along the top edge.

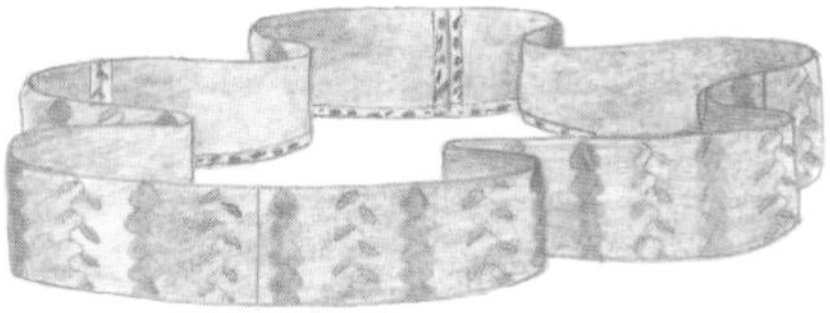

For a continuous frill, stitch short ends together.

Fabric Width Conversion Chart

35"–36"	44"–45"	52"–54"	58"–60"
90cm	115cm	140cm	150cm
1¾(1.60m)	1⅜(1.30m)	1⅛(1.10m)	1(1m)
2(1.90m)	1⅝(1.50m)	1⅜(1.30m)	1¼(1.20m)
2¼(2.10m)	1¾(1.60m)	1½(1.40m)	1⅜(1.30m)
2½(2.30m)	2⅛(2m)	1¾(1.60m)	1⅝(1.50m)
2⅞(2.70m)	2¼(2.10m)	1⅞(1.80m)	1¾(1.60m)
3⅛(2.90m)	2½(2.30m)	2(1.90m)	1⅞(1.80m)
3⅜(3.10m)	2¾(2.60m)	2¼(2.10m)	2(1.90m)
3¾(3.50m)	2⅞(2.70m)	2⅜(2.20m)	2¼(2.10m)
4¼(3.90m)	3⅛(2.90m)	2⅝(2.40m)	2⅜(2.20m)
4½(4.20m)	3⅜(3.10m)	2¾(2.60m)	2⅝(2.40m)

Double frill: For a double frill, you need twice the required width and twice the seam allowance. Fold the strip lengthways, wrong sides facing, and baste

Baste and gather both layers together.

Sewing tip

When instructions indicate that the seam allowance is to be added, first re-fold the fabric, right sides facing. Pin out the pattern. Draw round the outline of the pattern pieces using pencil or dressmaker's chalk pencil. (Add all marks etc.) Cut out ⅜in (9mm) from the pattern edge. Unpin the pattern. Baste the fabric pieces together, and stitch along the chalked line. This method enables you to achieve accurate stitching and perfect straight seams.

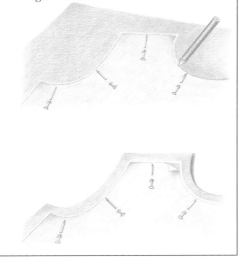

the raw edges together. Then gather and apply the frill as for the single frill, working both layers together. If you need to neaten the ends, fold the frill ends right sides facing and stitch across the ends. Trim the seam allowance and turn the frill right side out. Then gather and apply as for the single frill.

Binding edges

Bias binding is a neat way of finishing a raw edge as well as adding a touch of colour or pattern. Bias binding can be purchased ready-made in plain-coloured or patterned cotton or in acetate satin. If you wish to make your own bias binding, cut bias strips (see page 108). Press the sides of the strips to the centre by one quarter.

To bind the edge of a piece of fabric, unfold one edge of the binding and lay against the fabric with right sides facing. The crease of the fold lies along the seamline. Pin, baste and stitch in the crease. Trim the fabric edge a little and fold the binding over the edge to the wrong side. Baste, then slipstitch in place, working over the previous stitches.

If the binding is to be top-stitched, work the first stage of application in the same way. Bring the binding over the raw edge then baste and machine-stitch in place.

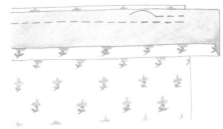

Open the binding and baste, then stitch along the fold line.

Fold the binding to the wrong side and slipstitch in place.